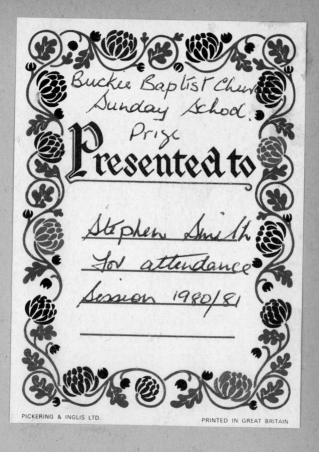

Buckie Baptist Church
Sunday School.
Prize

Presented to

Stephen Smith
For attendance
Session 1980/81

PICKERING & INGLIS LTD.   PRINTED IN GREAT BRITAIN

DEATH
OF
A
GURU

Rabindranath R. Maharaj

WITH

DAVE HUNT

HODDER AND STOUGHTON
LONDON SYDNEY AUCKLAND TORONTO

Wonderful, copyright 1924.
Renewed 1952 by Lillenas Publishing Co.
Used by permission

Contents

DEATH
OF
A
GURU

Prologue

It could hardly be said that my arrest on that blustery morning in November 1975, as I sought to cross the border from Pakistan into India, came as a complete surprise. The risk had been well understood, but my mission was of such importance that hesitation was unthinkable. And now it would do no good to worry over what could turn out to be just a short delay . . . or the inevitable that I had half feared.

I had been told to wait outside while my papers were being examined. During the ten minutes that I paced slowly back and forth in front of the austere border station under the cool gaze of several guards, I began to suspect what was coming. The longer I waited the more certain I became.

Preoccupied with my thoughts, I hardly noticed the officer approach me. "You are Rabindranath Maharaj?" he asked, comparing the photograph on my passport with my bearded features. Why the beard? he seemed to be thinking. Or perhaps it was, Of course, a beard!

"Yes, I am." I smiled pleasantly. It was a natural reaction, one which my friends expected and often commented upon. Yes, Rabi was such an amiable fellow. *Even at a time like this*, I thought. But I wasn't smiling inside.

"Come with me!" He turned abruptly and motioned for me to follow.

Inside the low frame building I was ordered into a back room where several other uniformed officials with grim expressions awaited me. It was there, away from the eyes of the few tourists who were passing the border with little delay in both directions, that I heard those chilling though half-expected words, "You are under arrest!" As though for the first time I became aware of how cold and hard the revolvers looked that each of the men surrounding me was wearing.

"Why are you spying for the Indian government?" The question came from the senior officer sitting behind the desk.

"But I'm not!" I protested.

"And you think we'll believe that, don't you," he said with a sarcastic laugh. "Did you really imagine we'd let you leave the country?"

Of course I was an Indian, and Indians didn't travel in Pakistan—not ordinarily, at least. Millions of them had fled this hostile land after it had come under Muslim control as a result of Partition, and thousands had been brutally slaughtered even as they tried to escape. On the other side of the border, Hindus had butchered thousands of Muslims as millions fled India for this haven carved out for them by the British as their last act before surrendering control of this vast portion of their dwindling empire. Since Partition there had been numerous border clashes between Indian and Pakistani troops; and India's recent intervention in the war between East and West Pakistan, resulting in the independence of Bangladesh would never be forgiven or forgotten. No Indian in his right mind would enter such hostile territory unless he had a very special mission. That was what my interrogators were thinking—and in fact they were correct.

There was incriminating evidence against me, so they implied, but it wasn't spelled out. That was part of the game —and I well knew there could be no defense against whatever accusations they made. My last name told these men that I was a member of the highest Hindu caste; and with such hostility between India and Pakistan, that fact alone was sufficient to support the charge. After all, what else would any Indian— especially a Brahmin—be doing in Pakistan except spying?

10

I had heard stories enough to know that I could expect no trial, no due process of law. In actual fact I was not a spy; although my mission in Pakistan, which had been completed successfully, would no doubt be considered just as hostile as espionage if it were known. Looking from one grim face to the other, seeing their rejection of my denials, I felt a sudden wave of hopelessness. This would surely be the last day of my life . . . and there was so much work yet undone.

There would be no news item, no formal announcement of my execution. I would simply disappear without a trace, and my mother waiting for me near Bombay, whom I had not seen for years, would never know what had happened or why. After a few official inquiries by my own government, and equally formal denials by the Pakistanis, I would soon be forgotten, one more casualty in that secret war that is never reported by the news media.

As I waited alone, under close guard, for the arrival from Lahore of the man they called the Chief—he wanted to interrogate me personally—I thought of one slim possibility for obtaining my release. It would involve convincing these hardened police of something they would find nearly impossible to believe. I had to give it a try, at least. Perhaps the very strangeness of the tale would be in my favor. Perhaps the Chief would see that it was all too unbelievable to be a lie.

To be understood, the incredible story would have to be told from the very beginning. going back to my early childhood in Trinidad.

ONE

The Avatar

No matter how fulfilling life becomes, there are always certain regrets when one looks back. My deepest sense of loss involves my father, Chandrabhan Ragbir Sharma Mahabir Maharaj. How I wish he were still alive! Nor does the fact that this extraordinary man died so young and under such mysterious circumstances entirely explain my regret. So much that is even more remarkable has happened since. I often wonder what it would be like to share it all with him, and what his reaction would be.

To share it with him! We never shared anything in our lives. Because of the vows he had taken before I was born, not once did he ever speak to me or pay me the slightest heed. Just two words from him would have made me unspeakably happy. More than anything else in the whole world I wanted to hear him say, "Rabi! Son!" Just once. But he never did.

For eight long years he uttered not a word, not even a whispered confidence to my mother. The trancelike condition which he had achieved is called in the East a state of higher consciousness and can be arrived at only through deep meditation—or by the ingestion of certain drugs like LSD. Such behavior may seem odd in the extreme to those unacquainted with Eastern mysticism. Western society, based as it is upon scientific materialism, traditionally regarded mystical experiences as some form of hallucination caused by superstition and ignorance. Recent scientific proof of psychic phenomena is slowly changing that attitude, bringing a growing open-mindedness to the occult. We Indians, however, have known for thousands of years that there is real power in Yoga. My father proved it. He was the ultimate exemplar in real life of what the yogis and gurus, now famous in Europe and America, teach. He lived what they talk about, as few men ever have.

"Why is Father that way?" I would ask my mother when I was still too young to understand.

"He is someone very special—the greatest man you could have for a father," she would reply, always patient with my persistent questions and puzzled expression. "He is seeking the true Self that lies within us all, the One Being, of which there is no other. And that's what you are too, Rabi."

With little understanding at first, nevertheless I soon came to believe that he had made the noblest of all choices. Mother often assured me of that, and so did many others. They said that Buddha's Great Renunciation hardly compared with my father's. When I was old enough to search the sacred writings I agreed. My father's renunciation had been complete—precipitously so, within days of his marriage. Had it occurred any sooner, I would not have been born.

Though I accepted the idea that a higher choice caused my father never to speak to me, his only child, I could not deny the gnawing emptiness, the intense longing, the peculiarly uncomfortable hunger that I learned to live with, even to ignore, but never conquered. Resentment, however, would have been unthinkable. To a Hindu, the *Bhagavad-Gita* is the Book of books, and my father had courageously chosen to live by it. How could I, with the religious training my mother had given me, be resentful of that? But I still felt the longing for his companionship.

No one, not even my mother, ever knew exactly the vows he had taken; they could only be surmised from the unusual style of life he suddenly adopted. Sitting in lotus position —toes of both feet turned up on top of the knees—on the

14

board that he also used for a bed, he passed his days in meditation and the reading of the sacred scriptures—nothing else. Mantras are a necessity for meditation; the vibrations they create are the chief way of attracting the deities, and without the aid of these spirit beings there is no real benefit to the meditator. But my father was beyond the use of mantras. We all considered him to be in direct communion with Brahman. So completely had he turned within to realize the true Self that he never acknowledged any human presence, although admirers came from miles around to worship him and to lay before him their offerings of fruit and flowers, cotton cloth, and money. No one ever aroused a response from him. He seemed to be in another world. Years later I would achieve a meditation deep enough to visit the secret universe of strange planets and Ascended Masters where my father apparently passed his time. To my disappointment, I never found him there.

But I'm getting ahead of the story. Such accomplishments do not come easily, nor are they explained easily to those who have experienced the universe only through the restrictive filter of the five senses. We must begin our journey slowly. The first step is to lay aside the prejudice of many years, especially the irrational insistence that anything we can't understand or detect with the crude instruments of today's technology cannot be real. Even what we think we know lies outside those limits; for who understands what life is, or energy, or even light? And what instrument can measure love?

Even as a small boy, a fierce pride stirred within me whenever I heard my father praised, which was often indeed. With awe and respect, religious Hindus spoke of him as one who had the courage and conviction to tread higher and mysterious paths. In the opinion of many, including the greatest pundit I ever knew, Father was an avatar. I heard that word for years before I really understood what it meant. How good it sounded—and so very special! I knew that *I* was special, too, because he was *my* father. One day I would be a great Yogi, too. A little-understood intuition at first, that conviction deepened with the passing years.

Never in my wildest dreams, however, could I have imagined the surprises that awaited me. There is so much that I wish now could be shared with my father—but he is gone.

How often I stood in front of this extraordinary man, staring into his eyes until I became lost in their fathomless depths. It was like falling through space, reaching out to grab something, calling for someone, but meeting only silence and emptiness. I knew then that he had found the Bliss that Lord Krishna offered to Arjuna. He looked so peaceful, sitting motionless, his breath moving in and out slowly, rhythmically, hair and beard, uncut in all those years, grown down to his waist. At such times I felt myself to be in the presence of a god.

We would move the god figures on the family altar tenderly, unwrapping them from the soft cloth, then covering them again; bathing them, clothing them with great care and reverence. It was like that with my father too. Like the gods in the prayer room, he did nothing physically for himself. He was a god to be taken care of, washed and fed and changed. For eight years. My father had followed Lord Krishna's instructions about giving up all attachments to position, desires, the physical realm. No wonder people marveled and came from far and near to worship him. It was often said in solemn, reverent tones that surely he had already achieved *moksha*, escaping the wheel of reincarnation. There would be no more births into this world of death for him, only the eternal Bliss of nirvana. He had entered that Highest Path, and I knew we would never meet again even before his mysterious death took us all by surprise.

"Vishnu he say he goin' go have an ambulance take him to the sanitarium!"

I was standing outside, eating a fresh mango I had just

plucked, when the words drifted on the still morning air through an open window. The voice was Phoowa Mohanee's, my father's elder sister and his most ardent disciple. She was inside helping my mother wash my father, whom she loved and worshiped with a passion. Vishnu was one of her close relatives, a successful businessman who had no time for religion and only harsh words for my father. Forgotten, the mango slipped from my fingers. I edged closer to the window, holding my breath to hear better.

The conversation, however, became muffled and indistinct amid rubbings and splashings. There was something about Vishnu insisting that my father would "come out of it quickly enough if people stopped treating him like a god." Incomprehensible words to my childish understanding, like "shock treatments" and "psychiatrist," filtered through the window, with more talk about doctors and medicine. It left me bewildered and frightened, especially to hear my mother's voice becoming almost as hysterical as Mohanee's. She was always so calm. Only something of the utmost gravity could so distress her.

Under the scattered coconut palms, I ran down the familiar path toward the two-room hut of mud walls and hard-packed dirt and cow-dung floor topped by corrugated tin roof that my mother's father, Lutchman Singh, had allowed an old family friend, Gosine, to build on part of his sprawling property not far from the house he had given to my parents as a wedding present. The thin, wiry old man, his skin wrinkled and weathered like ancient parchment, was in his usual position, squatting on his haunches on the bare earth in the meager shade of a cashew tree in front of the low hut, dhoti skirt tucked up between his legs, arms on knees, chin cupped in both hands.

"Why for you lookin' so sad, son of the Great Yogi?" Gosine asked, looking up at me with that wise expression that made it easy for me to believe that he was an ancient sage reincarnated and grown old once again.

"Why you think I so sad?" I responded defensively, falling easily into the Trinidadian village English Gosine spoke. It had become second nature to me, in spite of my mother's efforts to insist upon proper grammar. It was hopeless trying to purge me of the vernacular spoken by all my friends in our country town. "You ain't look so happy youself," I added for good measure.

"I ain't sleep good las' night, man. I feelin' like a dry-up old rag," said Gosine solemnly, his thick gray mustache bobbing up and down as he spoke. I wasn't sure which fascinated me more, that wobbly mustache or the long tufts of hair growing out of his ears.

I squatted beside him in silence. We were good friends, good enough that talking wasn't necessary, and I found comfort just being near him. It was several minutes before I found the courage to unburden myself. "You know what is a *sikatris*—or shock treatin'?"

Rubbing his chin contemplatively, the old man furrowed his brow in deep thought for some time before he answered. "Big-city talk—don't mean nothin' out here. Where you hearin' that stuff? On radio, must be."

"It was Vishnu. I didn't hear *him* exactly—"

"Vishnu not *bad*—jus' reckless. Mohanee not talk loud 'nuff. You father handle him all right. Them were the days. . . ."

I sat quietly again, disappointed. Gosine had always seemed so infallibly wise. Maybe it *was* big-city talk—but it had to mean something.

"I ain't never go get over that weddin'," he said abruptly, as though he were going to tell me something for the first time. In fact, I had heard the story from him at least twenty times, almost word for word.

"Boy, you father mighty clever man. And you is you father true, true son. You shoulda see the crown he wear at the weddin'. 'Lectric lights blinkin' all over it, join up to a batt'ry in his pocket. 'E 'vented it 'imself. You shoulda hear

18

them people when he step outa that car right in front of you Nana store!"

"You was there?" I asked innocently, as though I didn't know.

"Boy, I tellin' you what I see myself—this ain't no second-hand story. That was the bigges' weddin' I ever see, and the most 'spensive. If I was there! You think I goin' go miss *that?* Drums an' dancin' an' plenty eatin' and drinkin'. Food for so, boy, 'nuff to fill you up for a month. And the dowry! You shoulda see *that!* If you do as well as your father . . . hmm!"

He paused at this point, as he always did, then went on, but with a new note of awe in his voice. "And he give it all up! Ev'rythin'! You know somethin'? He's a avatar, you know!"

Gosine lapsed into silence to dramatize what he had just said, and I stood to leave. Ordinarily I would have stayed on to listen. Eventually he would have gotten past the wedding and perhaps started telling me a story from the *Mahabharata* or *Ramayana* about the adventures of the gods. He knew the Hindu religion and the favorite myths as well as anyone, and I had learned a lot from him. But I didn't want to hear any more talk about my father, especially about how wonderful he was. I sensed that something awful was going to happen, and it only made me feel more apprehensive to hear Gosine praise him.

Several days passed without any unusual events, and I began to forget about Vishnu's threat. It had not been clear to me anyway, and I had been afraid to ask my mother about it. Life was full of mysteries, many of them too awesome to talk about.

My mother was a beautiful woman of fine features, highly intelligent and possessed of an unusual inner strength. Her marriage to my father had been arranged by their parents, of course, in the traditional Indian manner. Only fifteen at the time and at the top of her class in school, looking forward

19

eagerly to pursuing her education, she was taken by surprise when her father gave her in marriage. Ended were her dreams of university in England. She became ill with the shock but submitted, nevertheless, to her father's will. Two of the most important pundits in the area read the young couple's palms, consulted the stars and a book of wisdom in such matters, and declared that the union would have the blessing of the gods. My mother may have felt otherwise, but who would dare to question what the stars had decreed and the pundits declared? Nor would she disappoint her parents by showing any signs of unhappiness. Among Hindus, duty to family and caste is sacred.

That obedience was rewarded almost immediately by an even greater shock when her husband, without warning, abruptly withdrew into a world of silent meditation. Even his eyes no longer communicated with those around him. I can scarcely imagine the consternation it must have created in my mother, a young bride of fifteen and pregnant, to face her responsibilities—which now included caring for her husband as she would for a child born deaf, dumb, and blind. But she never complained, and as I grew older I witnessed her tender care and steadfast loyalty to my father. She seemed blessed with a sympathetic understanding of the path he had chosen.

Quiet, meditative, and deeply religious, she was not only father and mother to me but also my first teacher in Hinduism. How well I remember those early lessons learned as a little child sitting close beside her in the family prayer room in front of the altar with its numerous gods! The heavy scent of sandalwood paste freshly marked on the deities, the flickering *deya* flame attracting my eyes like a magnet, and the solemn sound of softly repeated mantras created an aura of holy mystery that held me spellbound. From the many millions of Hindu gods our family had chosen its favorite deities; and as a small child, even before I understood what they represented, I sensed and feared the power of the small figures standing on the altar and the pictures on the wall around which we hung the sacred beads. Those unblinking eyes of clay and wood and brass and stone and painted paper seemed to watch me when I was not watching. In some strange way these impassive figures seemed more alive than I was and possessed miraculous powers that held us all in awe. Our offerings and worship acknowledged this fearsome superiority.

When the morning or evening *puja* was done, mother and I would linger together after aunts and uncles and cousins had returned to their worldly cares and duties. She would teach me diligently how to be, first of all, a Hindu steadfast in devotion to the gods and unfailing in my religious duties. All else was secondary. It was from her lips that I first understood that I, because of past karma, had been born into the highest caste. I was a Brahmin, a representative on earth of Brahman, the One True Reality. Indeed, I *was* Brahman—it only remained for me to realize this, my true Self.

As though the more than twenty years since then were only twenty days, I can still hear her soft, clear voice quoting Lord Krishna from favorite passages in the *Bhagavad-Gita*.

> Let the Yogi constantly engage in Yoga, remaining in a secret place by himself, with thought and self subdued, free from hope and greed. With thought and senses subdued, steady on his seat, he should practice Yoga for the purification of the self. Holding the body, head, and neck erect, immovable, steady, looking fixedly at the point of the nose ... firm in the vow of the Brahmacharya, the mind controlled, thinking on Me ... the Yogi ever united thus with the Self ... goeth to Peace, to the supreme Bliss that abideth in Me.

Krishna was the Master and Originator of true Yoga, as the *Gita* said, and my father was his truest disciple. With the swiftly passing years, this understanding deepened within me, until I became a Yogi myself.

Following such instructions from my mother's lips, and

guided by my father's perfect example, from the age of five I practiced meditation daily. Sitting in lotus position with my spine straight and my eyes staring unseeing at nothing, I imitated the one who by then seemed more like a god than a father to me.

"You look so much like your father when you meditate!" my mother would sometimes tell me quietly, with obvious pride in her voice. "You will be a great Yogi too, one day!" The tender words deepened my determination not to disappoint her.

Though she was so very young, Mother had shouldered her unusual responsibilities alone. She had not wanted her wealthy father to know that she sometimes had to beg the water that neighbors cooked their rice in to feed me when I was a tiny infant. Grandfather Singh, whom we called Nana, eventually found out and insisted that Mother move back into the family house. Her sister Revati was always begging to live there. She would arrive periodically, with her growing troop of small children, tearfully asking shelter, showing the ugly bruises from the latest beating her husband, a heavy rum-drinker, had given her. Wife-beating was quite common, so after allowing Revati to recuperate for a few weeks, Grandfather always sent her back. After all, he had arranged for her to marry this man and had a reputation to maintain of standing by his word. Aunt Revati would inevitably reappear, bruised and beaten, children in tow, and of course pregnant. When she had given birth to the latest child, Grandfather would send her back to her husband again. After the fifth child, and my grandfather's death, Aunt Revati stayed on with us in the large family house. I enjoyed having my cousins there. Typical of Hindu joint families, there were usually fifteen or twenty of Nana's descendants living there together at any time—aunts, uncles, cousins, and Nanee, his widow, whom we all affectionately called "Ma."

Nana died when I was still very young. His was the bedroom my mother and I then shared. His rum shop and dry-goods store downstairs, and the large living quarters upstairs, still echoed with Nana's heavy, angry footfall long after his death. At such times his spirit could be felt brooding within that fortresslike mansion he had built of solid concrete. Those who do not believe in the occult forces underlying the universe may consider this to be rank superstition or hysteria. However, we *heard* his footsteps stomping back and forth in the attic, and often just outside our bedroom doors when we had retired for the night. Visitors, too, experienced these things. There was hardly a guest who spent the night with us who was not attacked physically by unseen hands or did not see sudden apparitions. Some relatives would never stay overnight again after one such experience. But those of us who called that house our home had no choice but to remain there.

Nana had been heavily involved in Hindu occultism and was critical of those who merely philosophized about their religion without learning to use the supernatural forces. As I grew older I learned that he had killed his first son, offering the tiny baby as a sacrifice to the gods. This was not an uncommon practice, but it was never spoken of openly. Nana's favorite deity was Lakshmi, consort of Vishnu the preserver. Goddess of wealth and prosperity, she demonstrated her great powers when Nana rose at almost one leap to become one of the most powerful and wealthy men in my native Trinidad. When the small frame shack Nana had built for his family and business mysteriously burned down, he had replaced it with a huge house that became a landmark on the road from Port of Spain to San Fernando. No one could guess where the money had suddenly come from—or where he had acquired the gold that he stacked in the large safe sunk into a think concrete wall of the new house. Not many of the hundreds of thousands of emigrants from India and their descendants had been able to accumulate wealth so easily and so suddenly. We all knew that powerful gods had helped him. In turn he had given his soul to them.

Lutchman Singh Junction, where I lived, had been named

after Nana. It lies on the main road about thirty miles south of Port of Spain. Among the large East Indian population in Trinidad, Nana was recognized as one of the Hindu leaders, a man who had mysterious supernatural powers that none could deny or cared to meddle with. It was common knowledge that spirits guarded the more than one million dollars in gold coins Nana had buried on one of his many properties—no one knew just where—at the beginning of World War II. Few would dare to defy the spirits by seeking that buried treasure, and there was not an obeah man who had been able to learn the secret location using even his most potent sorceries. Those priceless gold coins, worth many times as much today, remain hidden still.

Nana prized occult power even more highly than money. His strong iron safe contained one object he wouldn't sell at any price—a small white stone from India, possessed of spirit powers both to heal and to curse. It would draw the venom out if held over a snakebite, so reliable witnesses reported, although I never observed that particular feat myself. One of my uncles told me how, out of curiosity, he had once cautiously opened the door of the private room containing Nana's safe . . . to be greeted by a giant snake that guarded not only the money and papers but other secrets of that room that were only speculated about in whispers. Whether the snake was real or a form taken by the spirits, as some have suggested, I myself saw that huge brightly colored reptile lurking under the house long after Nana's untimely death of a heart attack at the age of fifty.

To the Hindu, snakes are gods. I kept a live one—a splendid macajuel snake—in my room and worshiped it, just as I worshiped the monkey god and the elephant god and above all the cow god. For me, God was everything and everything was God—except, of course, those unfortunate beings who had no caste. My world was filled with spirits and gods and occult powers, and my obligation from childhood was to give each its due.

24

This was the culture that bred my father. He had perfectly followed in the footsteps of Krishna and the other great Yogis who had gone before, and my mother taught me that I must do the same. That was something I never doubted. Father had set an example, achieved wide acclaim, and earned the worship of many, and it was inevitable that upon his death his mantle would fall upon me. I had never imagined, however, that I would still be so young when this fateful day ordained of the gods would overtake me.

"Please come with us, Rabi!" my cousins begged. Uncle Kumar was taking them to the nearby beach at Monkey Point for a swim. It was always an honor to have a Brahmin in the party, an almost certain assurance of good luck. I was treated like a prince and felt like one.

"Not today," I said, shaking my head firmly. I had determined to finish an intricate religious picture I was drawing.

"Please!" pleaded Sandra and Shanti together.

"I can't!" No further explanation was needed. Everyone in the household knew that for me religious duty and devotion came first. I would sit by the hour drawing pictures of my favorite gods—Hanuman, Shiva, Krishna, Ganesha, and others. Already I was a mystic, feeling a oneness with the deities, willing to sacrifice going to the beach for a swim or playing in the yard and nearby fields with friends, choosing instead to devote myself to making my gods. Coloring them lavishly, I would hang them on the walls in my room to keep them close to me, worshiping them, determined to devote my life to Hinduism, which my mother had taught me was the oldest and greatest and only true religion.

Mother, who always took me when she went to care for my father—he was now living with his half-sister, Mohanee—had gone off to see him without me. It had been a disappointment, putting me in a brooding mood. Contemplation of the gods I had drawn, however, cheered me. With small brown fingers clutching the crayons, I carefully colored my drawing of Vishnu. How pleased Mother would be on her return to see the four-handed Narayana lying on the coils of Ananta the serpent, attended by Lakshmi and Brahma, the latter sitting on a lotus issuing from Vishnu's navel . . . all riding on a tortoise floating on the primal sea.

Adding a touch here, erasing a smudge there, satisfied with my work, I was chanting softly, "*OM*, Shiva; *OM*, Shiva; *OM*, Shiva," when I heard my mother's familiar footsteps hurrying up the outside stairway. The door to the kitchen burst open, immediately followed by the babble of excited voices. I started from the room but was stopped in the doorway by what I heard.

"He's dead! Chandrabhan's dead!" I stood rooted to the spot. Everyone began talking at once and I missed the next few words.

"I had a bad feeling when I got up this morning." My mother's voice was heavy with grief, but clear and strong. "I hurried right there. Just as I arrived the nurse began to cut his hair. The doctor had ordered it."

"But why was he in a hospital?" my Aunt Revati demanded. "He wasn't ill, was he?"

"This was Vishnu's doing. Chandrabhan looked like always—strong and serene within himself."

There was a long pause, then Mother recovered her voice and continued. "They cut his hair—the doctor said it was too long to keep sanitary in the hospital. And when they cut it . . . he . . . he fell backward. I ran to him. We tried to give him some water—but the doctor said he was dead. Can you believe it? Like *that!*"

I ran to my bed, fell across it, and buried my face in a pillow, trying to muffle the gasps and wails that heaved my chest and burst from my throat. I felt that I had lost everything. Though I had scarcely known him as my father, he had been my inspiration, a god—an avatar—and now he was dead. I had known it was coming, felt it inside of me when Gosine had talked about the wedding again that day. Now it had happened, and I would never hear him speak. There were so many questions I had wanted to ask, so much he must have known that I had hoped one day to learn from his lips. Most of all I had wanted to hear him call my name, tell me I was his son. Now that dream was dashed forever.

From sheer exhaustion my sobs subsided at last. I lay quietly for a long time, trying without much success to comprehend Krishna's words to Arjuna as he sent him into battle. My mother had repeated them to me so often that I knew them by heart: "The wise grieve neither for the living nor for the dead . . . nor verily shall we ever cease to be. . . . The dweller in the body . . . passeth on to another body; the steadfast one grieveth not thereat."

With the slow, erratic footsteps of a man carrying a heavy burden, my Uncle Kumar came into the room to announce my father's death, not realizing that I already knew. My mother was too overwrought to tell me. He thought that I bore the news bravely, unaware that I was already too wearied with sorrow to show it outwardly any longer.

My father's sudden and mysterious death was, of course, a great shock not only to the family but to all who knew him. The doctors could find no medical explanation. He had been in perfect health. Had he achieved Self-realization and his spirit taken flight, escaping the wheel of reincarnation? I wanted to believe it. But some thought that the spirits had taken his life for breaking his vows. That seemed unfair to me. It had not been his doing but that of others—of Vishnu who had sent him to the hospital and of the doctors who were not Hindus and had no knowledge of the power of the occult forces or of the vow of the Brahmacharya. My father had been sincerely following Krishna's instructions in the *Bhagavad-Gita*. Vishnu should have known, he who had been raised in a Hindu family and taught well. But he had thought that the life of a Yogi was a farce, that the gods and the spirit powers were only the product of the pundits' imagination and some clever tricks. I would not make the same mistake. My faith in Hinduism would never waver. We had all learned not to despise what we could not understand, but it had been a costly lesson.

When we arrived at Phoowa Mohanee's house my eyes carefully avoided the rough wooden casket perched on a table in the living room. In the presence of death every ritual must be closely observed and no fire could be lit in that house, no food cooked while the deceased rested there before moving on in his journey to other worlds. While the pundit led a long *puja*, friends and relatives wailed, and Phoowa, my father's most ardent disciple, outdid all the rest in the fervor of her grief. I cowered beside my mother, shrunk within myself in childish defense against my role as one of the central figures in a drama beyond my comprehension. After the ceremony a kindly neighbor took me gently from my mother's side and led me to the coffin.

"There is your father," she said, as though I didn't know. How I shrank from being reminded.

Oddly, this god, this avatar, that I had so often stood before and stared at with such intense longing, seemed no more remote in death. The expression was almost the same, but the face was so very pale. Brahmins, who are descended from the early Aryans, are generally of lighter skin than other Indian castes, and my father had been exceptionally light even for a Brahmin. Now he looked as white as an Englishman, and the closed eyelids were like wax. I turned away and pulled free from her hand.

The funeral procession was a long one, for my father had been greatly beloved and revered by religious Hindus for miles around. Cars and bicycles and oxcarts carrying mourners were strung out along the narrow road leading to the coast just two miles to the west. I was too bewildered and frightened to ask Mother why we weren't going to the cemetery where my two grandfathers had been buried so recently. Why were we heading toward Monkey Point where we always went swimming? The question only added to the feeling of mystery surrounding my father's death, but I kept it inside of me and gripped my mother's hand more tightly.

Carefully avoiding the coffin sitting askew in the funeral coach ahead, I fixed my attention instead upon the tall sugarcane on either side of the narrow road, watching it slip slowly by, motionless and solemn, the long yellowish leaves drooping as though in sadness. That was as it should be, since all things in the universe—human, animal, inanimate—had a common Being. It seemed to me that the whole of nature mourned the passing of the avatar. When would another such divine manifestation appear in human form? Even the pundits —those Brahmins of great understanding—didn't know.

Hanging heavy and hot, the air seemed oppressively still for a land usually swept by the ceaseless current of trade winds. Ahead on the horizon, beyond the Gulf of Paria, I could see dark clouds hovering over the familiar Dragon's Mouth, where the northern tip of my native Trinidad jutted west, straining to touch the nearby Venezuelan coast. How often I had run and skipped down this familiar narrow lane, laughing with cousins and young friends on our way to a swim, my temples throbbing with the warmth of life, exulting in youthful joy, feeling a part of each familiar landmark along the way. Now I felt a frightening numbness inside and a bewildering separation from the workers who looked up curiously from the cane fields as the long procession slowly passed. They were part of another world to which I had once belonged.

Leaving the cane fields behind, the procession followed the road across the wide mangrove swamp running up and down the western side of the island. We parked on the graveled fill that stood just above the lapping waters of the small bay, which was protected from storms by a low concrete retaining wall. On holidays and after school, the larger boys would jump from the wall into the shallow water and swim out from shore. I was too small for that yet and would splash with my young friends behind the parking area in a shallow pool near the mangroves. How unreal the happy memories associated with this familiar and beloved place seemed now. I shivered as we stepped from the car, in spite of the hot sun.

The plain board coffin was pulled from the hearse and carried toward the edge of my swimming hole. Phoowa's pundit led the way, chanting in Sanskrit the Vedic mantra for driving away evil spirits. Following close behind the coffin, holding tightly to my mother's hand, I noticed for the first time a great pile of firewood neatly stacked on the gravel beside the small pool. The familiar mourners' wail once again filled the air, rising and falling in a chilling cadence. I watched in horror as my father's stiff body was lifted from the coffin and placed on the pile of logs. More firewood was quickly stacked around him until only his face remained visible, staring sightless at the sky. With sandalwood paste the pundit carefully made the last caste mark on the exposed forehead. Could it be—? Ritual burnings were a common sight in India along the Ganges at Benares and other cremation ghats, but I had never witnessed the practice among the Hindus in Trinidad. The thought of my father's body being given as a sacrifice to Agni, the god of fire, added a new dimension of mystery to the bewilderment and deep sense of loss that already overwhelmed me.

Rice was being prepared nearby to be offered to the deceased. The priest continued to rid the area of evil spirits, considered a necessary precaution before the fire god would release the spirit from the body and escort it to regions beyond. I stared with unseeing eyes at the methodical ritual being enacted before me.

"Come, Rabi!" It was the pundit's voice reminding me that I had a part to play, too.

Preoccupied with grief and fright, I had scarcely heard the mantras and had not seen him approach me with the sacred flame burning on a large brass plate balanced on one palm. With the other hand he reached out and took one of mine. I glanced apprehensively at my mother. She nodded and patted me on the shoulder. Bending low she whispered in my ear, "It's your duty. Do it bravely."

My eyes avoided my father's face as the pundit drew me over to the cremation pyre. Three times he led me around the corpse, reciting for me in Sanskrit the appropriate prayer because I was so young: "I apply fire to all limbs of this person, who, willingly or unwillingly, may have committed lapses and is now under the clutches of death . . . may he attain to shining regions." Now I could see the camphor cubes placed strategically here and there among the logs. Their pungent odor filled my nostrils. A tall, turbaned man in a dhoti began to sprinkle the ghee and kerosene over the logs and body. Following the pundit's instructions mechanically, I lit a brand in the sacred fire he held, then touched it to the nearest camphor. The flame sputtered, then grew and crept swiftly along the streaks of kerosene from one camphor cube to another. Fiery phantoms of red and yellow were soon dancing their ritual around the body. I stood there dazed as the flames leaped higher, until the pundit pulled me away.

Frantically I searched that sea of faces surrounding the flames and tried to choke back the sobs. Mother was nowhere to be seen. It was impossible to suppress the anguish I felt. Out it gushed in childish duplication of the wailing sounds all around me. I was half hysterical when at last I saw her standing near the burning body, so close that she seemed almost a part of the fire, her white silk sari silhouetted against the leaping orange flames. I had heard of widows throwing themselves on the pyre. Was I going to lose my mother as well as my father?

"Mommy!" I screamed. "Mommy!"

If she heard me above the roar of sparks and fire and the deafening din of mourning, she made no indication. Motionless she stood on the very edge of the inferno, her hands outstretched, worshiping the burning body and Agni, the all-consuming fire god. Bowing low, she threw offerings of the freshly cooked rice into the fire, then retreated from the unbearable heat and came to stand beside me. Head erect, she did not join in the mournful wailing. A true Hindu, she found strength to follow the teaching of Krishna: she would mourn neither the living nor the dead. Not once did she cry out during the hours we stood watching the dying flames. I sensed only that she prayed very quietly, as desperately I clung to her.

We kept our vigil until sunset. Then seven chips of wood were thrown into the embers, and the whole company of mourners marched round and round pouring offerings of water on the coals. At last the ashes were cool enough for the pundit to gather some of my father's bodily remains for Mother to carry to India to sprinkle on the sacred waters of the Ganges. How and when that would happen, I didn't know. I was already too bewildered and grief-stricken to give it any thought that night.

I had known an avatar—one of the gods in human form —and now he was gone. He had come to show men the path to follow, the path of true Yoga that yokes one with Brahman. I would not forget his example. I could not. His mantle had fallen on me, and I would follow in his footsteps.

TWO

Ashes on the Ganges

Like a flaming missile shot from Agni's bow, the sun, which I had just worshiped for an hour, arched higher into the sky behind me, throwing a pattern of shadow and light on earth and grass beneath the coconut palms. Leaving the veranda, I walked down the outside stairs and out to the shed where we kept the cow that provided our household with milk. Swinging the wooden gate open, I grabbed the trailing rope as the happy creature set off at a clumsy trot toward the pasture. She looked forward to her morning grazing as eagerly as I did. Half dragged along at the end of the rope, I managed somehow to guide the lurching animal to an oasis of fresh grass. Overhead, the broad branches of the coconut palms sang a familiar song as they gently brushed each other in the early morning breeze coming in from the bay. Head down, the cow busied itself as I watched reverently.

No creature is so venerated by Hindus as the cow. Sacred cow. Holy cow. Nose buried in the long grass, oblivious of all else, this black and white spotted deity with the twitching ears and switching tail tore huge mouthfuls of the juicy green carpet and chewed contentedly. Grazing the cow was my favorite pastime, and I gladly took advantage of my daily chore to worship this great and holy god. From the nearby profusion of a hibiscus, I plucked an orange blossom and placed it on the cow's head between her curved horns. She looked at me out of one brown eye, then continued to munch the grass. Disturbed by a fly crawling into one nostril, she shook her head and sneezed. The flower offering I had so carefully placed slid down her long nose onto the ground. Before I could retrieve it, the bright bloom had vanished along with a choice clump of grass. Sinking to the ground with a sigh, I tried to imagine what it would be like to be a cow. Perhaps I had already been one in a past life. I couldn't remember. I often wondered why I had no recollection of former lives.

Gosine had often told me how an ancient sage in faraway India had been the first one to see that most wondrous sight in the night sky, the shape of a cow outlined by a cluster of stars. According to Gosine, that was how we Hindus first learned that the cow was a god. I had heard other explanations involving Egypt and the Aryans, but Gosine's appealed to me the most. Anything in the heavens is holy; and of course all the cows on earth, having come from that one in the sky, were therefore worthy to be worshiped. Cow worship had progressed far since those early days. Gosine spoke of "Mother Cow," and I had often heard it said by the pundits that she was the mother of us all, just as Kali, the consort of Shiva, was. Somehow I knew that they must be one and the same, only in different form. Kali, my Aunt Revati's favorite deity, was so frightening, drinking fresh blood from a goblet, with garlands of freshly severed heads and hands hanging around her, standing on the prostrate form of her husband, Shiva. I much preferred worshiping the One Reality in the gentler form of the cow. And I was building good karma for my next life by spending so much time in our cow's company. Did she know she was a god? I watched her closely but discovered no clue to her self-awareness. Eventually the question was lost in the wonder and reverence I felt for this holiest of all creatures.

My adoration of the cow was interrupted by a faint humming sound that gradually grew louder and louder. Excited, I jumped to my feet and ran out from under the palms to get a better view. We saw very few airplanes in those days. Watching it pass reminded me of what I used to think when I was a little younger each time I saw a plane in the sky. Having pondered the mystery of my origin, I had finally asked my mother where I'd come from. Very seriously she had said, "You dropped out of the sky from an airplane one day, Rabi, and I caught you."

"Was I supposed to be yours?" I had asked, feeling suddenly insecure at the thought that I might just as well have landed in someone else's back yard.

Mother had assured me that I was meant to be hers and Father's. For months after that I had hoped for a baby brother to fall into my arms from a passing plane. Years later babies were still a mystery, but I was sure they didn't come from airplanes, and without understanding why, I knew that I would never have a brother or sister now that my father was dead.

Solemnly and faithfully I had worshiped his spirit every day since his passing. Each morning I had offered water to the special grass we had planted when he died, counting the days carefully as I watched it grow. Today was the fortieth day—and I would be losing my long, black, wavy hair, uncut for years, that everyone said made me look so much like my father. For days I had worried about being shorn. What if the spirits should take my life like they had taken my father's when his hair had been cut?

My mother was waving to me from the veranda. It was time for the ceremony. I began pulling at the rope, trying to drag the unwilling cow back to her shed. The poor creature dug in her heels and protested with grunts all the way. Firmness was required, but I would never prod her with a sharp stick or slap her with a switch as I had seen some of my young friends doing. "Is that any way to treat a god?" I had scolded on more than one occasion. And so they had learned to be more reverent—at least when I was watching.

It was a much smaller procession that followed the narrow asphalt road through the tall cane, past the mangrove swamp, to Monkey Point on the fortieth day after my father's death. All evidence of the cremation had been carried away by the tides that swept over the low concrete wall twice each day. Only the memory could not be erased. I saw again the leaping flames dancing their ritual around the body, smelled the burning flesh, and shuddered as I stood on the very spot where my father had been burned to ashes. Today, *I* was the center of attention.

Friends and relatives crowded around me in a small semi-circle as the pundit faced me with barber's scissors in one hand. The brief *puja* passed almost without my being aware. The present reality had been replaced by the sudden remembrance of a frightening experience. About three years before, I had been aroused from a sound sleep by hard, sharp, determined tugs on my hair. Fully awakened, I had writhed and twisted, shrieking with pain. Groping desperately, I had been unable to make flesh-and-blood contact with arms or hands, yet my hair was being pulled so hard that I was nearly dragged from my bed. My terrified screams had brought my mother to my side. With a few words and a pat on my back, she had assured me that it was a nightmare, nothing more. But I had known better. I had been wide awake, not dreaming, and the sharp pain where my hair had been nearly pulled out by the roots had lingered until morning.

That memory, together with the more recent one of my father's mysterious death, had frightened me as I anticipated this ceremony. But it passed uneventfully. Almost before I realized it, my hair had fallen to the ground where my father's ashes had lain. The next high tide would sweep those strands out to sea to join his remains.

Some of his ashes, however, had been saved for another special ceremony. Gosine and I had talked of it with considerable excitement several times since my father's death. "He was a avatar—no mistake," the old man had assured me. "It ain't no question of *moksha*. Not with *him!*"

"What you mean?" I had asked. "You don't think he reached *moksha?*"

"He done reach it long time—in some other life. This time he just come back to show the way . . . like Buddha, or Jesus."

"You mean he's one of the *Masters?*" I had been overcome at the thought.

Gosine had nodded emphatically. "You goin' go see on the fortieth day. It ain't go have no footprint on the ashes. No sah! His spirit took flight back to Brahman. He was a god, *Bhai*—that's who you father was!" Looking at me with awe, he had repeated those words in a deeply reverent tone. "That's who you father was!"

I had known it myself, standing before him when he was alive, looking into those deep eyes. But I hadn't understood it like Gosine did. He knew the Vedas even though he was uneducated. Gosine was a very smart man in my estimation, and a very knowledgeable Hindu.

Returning home, acutely conscious of my closely shorn head, I could hardly wait to verify what Gosine had said. The pundit led the way into an empty room that had been locked all night. In the center of the floor, filling a flat tray and carefully smoothed out, lay some of my father's ashes, reverently placed there the night before. Eagerly the family pressed forward to examine the surface for the telltale footprints that would reveal my father's latest reincarnation. It was a ceremony I had witnessed many times before, but I couldn't see the purpose now. My father was no longer on the wheel of reincarnation; he had returned to Brahman . . . so why bother with this ritual for him? I remembered Gosine's words: "It ain't go have no footprint on the ashes. No sah!"

I heard my mother gasp. Then the pundit exclaimed, "Hey, look! It have a bird foot! Right there!"

Words could not describe the consternation I felt. I pushed between my mother and aunt to see for myself. It was true! There in the center of the otherwise undisturbed surface of the ashes was the unmistakable imprint of a small bird's foot. We all examined it carefully. The conclusion was inescapable: my father had been reincarnated into a bird!

My small world was shattered. What would Gosine say now? But the island's chief pundit himself had called my father an avatar! If *he* hadn't attained oneness with Brahman, then what hope was there for me or for anyone else? I felt ill, unable to join in the babble of excited conversation as we all walked out to the yard together for the next part of this important ceremony.

Too numbed to think, I heard almost nothing of the long *puja*. I had no appetite for the huge feast that was to follow. For days the most delicious aromas had been tantalizing us from the kitchen, where my mother and aunts had been working long hours to prepare numerous favorite delicacies, curries, and sweets. Before anyone could take a taste, however, a sample of each kind of food had to be presented to the deceased. Filling a large dish made from the sacred koa leaf, the offering to my father's spirit was placed by the pundit at the base of a tall banana tree. Then we all turned to file back into the house.

"*Bhai ya*, nobody must look back, eh!" the pundit warned us solemnly. "If you look back the spirit could attack you. The offering is only for him alone."

Never could I have imagined myself violating that rule. But now I couldn't resist the temptation. Slowing my pace, I let the others pass me. He was *my* father. I must see him, if only once again. Just one peek! Halfway to the house, trembling with dread, yet unable to overcome the temptation, I glanced furtively over my shoulder. The leaf dish was still there, and I could plainly see the food in it. There was no sign of my father's spirit. Quickly I averted my gaze. I had committed the forbidden act! Now I was sure that each step I took would be my last. But nothing happened. Were the gods being merciful to me? I added this puzzle to the turmoil churning inside of me.

Hurrying onto the back veranda, I stood boldly on tiptoe to watch the barely visible dish. I had seen Yogi, the dog next door, eat the offering to Nana's spirit, and I wanted to be sure that didn't happen again. When perhaps half an hour had passed with no sign of anything unusual happening, I could restrain myself no longer. Still fearful of what the spirits might do, but somewhat bolder now, I returned to the yard and cautiously approached the banana tree. To my amazement, I found that the food was gone! Not a speck of it remained, yet I had seen nothing visible come near the dish! So it was true—my father's spirit had eaten it! Was this proof that he had not reached nirvana after all? Was he a bird in a tree, watching me now?

Despondent and confused, I stalked restlessly back and forth in the yard, searching the bushes and trees for a bird, small or large, that even faintly resembled my father. If I could not recognize him, at least he would know me. But I waited in vain for one of the flitting, chattering, preening creatures to pause and stare at me in recognition. None of them paid the slightest attention, unless I ventured too close, and then they flew away in fright. Of course my father had never paid any attention to me before he died, so why should he now?

Later I made my way down the familiar path to Gosine's hut. It had been impossible to talk with him alone when so many others were present His son, who was about forty, was out in front repairing a tire for his bicycle, which he pedaled around the town selling curry *channa* and *bara* made with red hot peppers. He had recently married a woman with two children, and they had all moved into the two-room hut with Gosine. Seeing me approach, he straightened up wearily from the flat tire, put both palms together in front of his chin, and bowed toward me.

"Sita-Ram," he said pleasantly. "You lookin' for the old man? He inside. He feelin' he old age."

"That ain't true, man!" responded Gosine's voice from

within. "I not feelin' nothin' like you say. The cold have me down." To prove his point, the proud old man, tall for an Indian and slightly bowlegged, came hobbling out to squat in his usual place in the protective shade of his hut. I squatted in silence. Just being beside him brought a comfort and sense of security that I couldn't explain.

"You nice hair go grow back fast," he said, shaking his head slowly from side to side like an upside-down pendulum.

"My hair ain't troublin' me," I replied, unable to share my inner turmoil and doubts.

"You know suthin', *Bhai*, I never go get over how you father live. The holiest man I ever know in m'whole life. . . the way he give up ev'rythin'!" Gosine's head continued to bob back and forth in astonishment.

Such praise had always made me swell with pride—he was *my* father—but now it gave me little comfort, even though I sensed that Gosine had now transferred to me the admiration he had felt for my father. The footprint of that tiny bird distinctly outlined in the ashes could not be denied. Everyone, even the pundit, had accepted it, apparently without the shock and disappointment I felt. That made my confusion all the more painful.

"How he so small now?" I asked. It would be easier to understand him becoming a large bird, but one so *small* only increased my bewilderment.

"Look, *Bhai, he* ain't small!" Gosine shot back emphatically. He became silent, rubbing his chin reflectively, then let out a long, loud sigh. "Hear what I say, eh. No bird with foot that small go eat that much food so *fast*."

Of course! Jumping to my feet, I ran back to that room where the ashes had been locked. Had we remembered to close the window tightly? I couldn't recall. Outside I looked up under the eaves and noticed the nest of a small bird. There was a series of semicircular holes one after the other where the rippling corrugated metal roof met the wall; large enough, I noted with excitement, for the tiny bird to enter the room.

But had the nest been there before my father had died? I couldn't be entirely sure, but it seemed to me that it had.

Then my father had left no footprint on the ashes after all! What a relief! But what about the food—who or what had eaten that? Perhaps one of the Asuras or Rakshasas, the demons the Vedas talked about, had interfered, trying to confuse us. That was it! But my father would protect me from these evil forces—he and the other Ascended Masters. I would believe in my father and what he had done. And I would follow in his footsteps.

"Rabi! Where are you? Baba is here!" Nanee was calling me.

"Coming, Ma!" I hurried up the stairs into the house where everyone was enthusiastically greeting our good friend.

"Rabi!" exclaimed the great man, squeezing me in a warm embrace. Jankhi Prasad Sharma Maharaj, a native of India, was the chief pundit on the island. There was no greater honor than having him visit in the home. A close friend and admirer of my father's, Baba stopped in every time he passed our house in the course of his travels, criss-crossing the length and breadth of Trinidad. He spoke mainly Hindi—very little English—and was well versed in Sanskrit. Tall, fair-skinned, and fairly stout, with a flowing beard turning white, he could have passed for Santa Claus had he been a bit fatter. An awesome figure to some, he was as jolly and friendly with me as Santa ever could be, and we loved one another.

"Rabi!" he exclaimed again, holding me at arm's length. "I see your father in you more and more every day. Bhagwan has his eyes on you. One day you will be a great Yogi! You have your father's eyes—and you'll have his hair again, too," he added with a laugh, affectionately running his fingers through my short hair that seemed to be growing so slowly.

He turned to my mother, who was beaming with pride beside me. "He's very special. *Very* special!" he repeated, shaking his head from side to side for emphasis. "One day he'll be a great Yogi like his father." My chest swelled and my eyes moistened. Yes, I *would* be. I stood as tall as I could.

This visit was a brief one. He was on his way to perform a special *puja* for a very wealthy Hindu in Port of Spain who had been stricken with cancer and wanted the way prepared —for a handsome fee—for his entrance into the next life. Some pundits, for the right price, even promised nirvana. Pundit Jankhi made no such guarantees, but thousands of Hindus had great faith in the efficacy of his intercession with the *devatas* and were willing to pay well to receive it.

After giving us his blessing, the great pundit gathered his dhoti closer about him and swept across the floor to the door, where he paused to bow. Hands in front of our faces, palms pressed together, we all bowed toward him in recognition of the deity in each of us. Another moment and he was hurrying down the stairs. I ran out onto the veranda and waved as he climbed into the car that was waiting for him. His words were still echoing in my ears when his car disappeared around the first curve. It was impossible for me to forget that I was special. Everyone reminded me of the fact. I *would* be a great pundit: more than that, a Yogi, a holy man like my father.

Mother had been standing beside me waving, too. Now she put her arm around me and patted my shoulder. I thought I knew what she was thinking. I would carry on for my father; his mantle had fallen upon me. She and I would follow in his footsteps together.

But I was mistaken. She was thinking of something else and trying to find words to soften the blow.

"Your father's ashes must be taken to the Ganges, Rabi," she said at last, "and spread on that holiest of all rivers to be carried out to sea. I would want you to do the same for me when I die."

The Ganges! What an aura of mystery surrounded that name. Holy Mother of rivers—like the cow, the Mother of us all, flowing pure out of the highest reaches of the Himalayas down the long steppes and valleys to the Bay of Bengal. At

Benares, the most Holy City, the ashes must be sprinkled on the waters. It would be the final committal of father's soul to the arms of Krishna.

"You will take me, won't you, Mommy?" I begged. "Please! Please, Mommy! I mus' go with you! You have to take me!"

"I would like to, Rabi, but it's too far for you. You'd get tired. And of course you can't miss school. . . ."

"I wouldn't get tired, I promise! And I could go to school in India."

She shook her head slowly and sadly. "I'm sorry . . . but don't worry, I'll come back soon. I promise."

"Please don't leave me!" I pleaded. "I don't want to stay here all alone without you!"

"You won't be alone. There's Ma and Aunt Revati and all your cousins and Uncle Kumar and Lari. . . ." She put her arm around me and patted my shoulder. "I'll be back soon, Rabi. That's a promise. What would you like me to bring you from India?"

"An elephant!" I said very earnestly. "One just like in the pictures!"

Mother had taught me that to accept whatever fate brought, without complaint, was my duty as a Hindu. But that duty of stoic acceptance of my karma, imposed upon me by Lord Krishna, became a burden too heavy for a small boy to bear when at last the day came for my mother to leave. Sadly I climbed into the car beside her for the drive to the docks at Port of Spain where she would board the ship that would take her to England and then on to India. Ma, who couldn't come with us, waved through the window and my mother waved back as we drove away on that saddest of all days. I waved good-bye, too, determined that I would go to India with her. In the stiff breeze, the latest Hanuman flag whipped back and forth on top of its pole in front of the rum and dry-goods shop. Cut out of white cloth and sewed lovingly by Ma to the red cotton background, the figure of my favorite hero, Hanuman the monkey god, seemed to be waving farewell to me. A good omen!

About a dozen carloads of relatives and friends came along to say farewell to my mother. It was less than a year since many of us had been at this same wharf to see my Uncle Deonarine off to England. He was my mother's eldest brother and had left to attend London University. Deonarine had been like a father to me. We had all stood on the quay and cried as the ship moved slowly out of the harbor. I had felt then that my heart would break. And now my mother was leaving. Furtively I wiped my eyes with a sleeve. I wanted to be brave, but the repeated reminder of relatives and friends of how privileged my mother was to make this holy pilgrimage became unendurable. "Your mother's going to India, Rabi, to the Ganges! She lucky for so, boy!" they kept saying. "Don't look so sad. She go come back soon." How could I tell them, or her, that my heart was breaking?

We all went aboard. Numbly I listened to the enthusiastic comments: how large and luxurious the ship was, how comfortable the accommodations, and the food—how exciting the foreign cuisine of this Dutch ship. It was all so ridiculous. What did my mother care for luxury? And as for the food, she sent one of my uncles down onto the dock to buy her a large supply of fruits and vegetables for the journey. Quite voluntarily, at the age of only four, I had made my own earnest promise to follow ahimsa, the principle of nonviolence, respecting all life—becoming a strict vegetarian like my mother. How dare friends and relatives imagine that she would even sit in the same dining room where the meat of the sacred cow was being devoured by unbelievers!

My religious zeal was not only to please the gods and to follow in my father's footsteps but to please my mother, who had taught me Hinduism. We were so very close, and I loved her so much. It was not right that I should be separated from her, I who followed the Hindu ideal far more closely than all of these loud well-wishers exclaiming so foolishly over the prospect of this voyage that brought me such pain.

The ship's whistle blew a long, loud blast. "Good-bye . . . have a good trip . . . write soon . . . good-bye . . . we'll miss you!" Everyone was trying to get in a last word.

"Give your mommy a kiss, Rabi!" Aunt Revati was nudging me forward. The reality of the loneliness I faced crashed in upon me.

"I'm goin' go to India, too!" I cried, grabbing with both hands the knob of the door to my mother's cabin and holding on with a death grip.

Kaka Nakhi, who used to chauffeur Nana around in his big yellow Chevrolet convertible, held out a bag of fresh peanuts. I loved them. "Here, Rabi," he said to mollify me. "Take them." But I wasn't going to be tricked. There was no way they would get me to let go of that door.

Mother began to plead with me. "Rabi, please! This isn't like you. Let go now. Go along with Aunt Revati. You can wave to me from the dock."

I tightened my grip. "I goin' go with you, Mommy! Please! Take me with you!"

"Come, come. We have to go!" said Aunt Revati, her eyes filled with tears at the thought of losing her sister. "The ship go leave us now." She tried gently to take my hand from the doorknob, but my grip was powered by fear. I saw the bewilderment on my mother's face. It would be unthinkable to force or to hurt me. I was the child saint, a Brahmin, son of a great Yogi. But the ship's whistle blew another warning blast.

"You've got to leave—*right now!*" It was my Uncle Kumar, towering over me, trying to be gentle but firm. Legal counselor for our county, his voice always carried a certain ring of authority. But I was determined and started to scream, holding on desperately. Kaka Nakhi joined Kumar in trying to take my hands gently from the doorknob. One hand was pulled free. Back it went again when the other was pried loose. My screams added to the confusion. "I goin' go with Mommy! I goin' go with Mommy!"

Never had I acted this way before. This small child saint was causing a shocking commotion before the thunder-struck relatives. But there was no more time to waste. Together Lari and Nakhi wrenched me away from the door and out of my mother's room. Kicking and screaming, I was carried off the ship and down onto the dock.

What a farewell! All the fight had gone out of me now. I stood sobbing, unable to see my mother's waving figure through the tears as the ship pulled away from the dock. All the way home I sobbed inconsolably. That night I cried my-self to sleep. The following day I refused to eat, sobbing hysterically in spite of every effort to comfort me. I knew that I should submit to whatever my karma brought upon me, but I was just a small boy, a very human one, who needed the love that only a mother could give.

I would never see her again. It was a terrible conviction which grew with each convulsive sob.

THREE

Karma and Destiny

"You must learn patience, Rabi. There are few things more important . . . or more difficult."

"But Ma, how Mommy say she go come back *soon?* Is a'ready two years, and now in she letter she say next year again. Ev'ry time is *next year!*" I still told friends who asked that she would return "next year," but I could no longer believe it myself.

Nanee was sitting in her usual seat beside the window where I visited her each morning. Bowing low with palms pressed together, I would then seat myself cross-legged on the floor in front of her. I watched her fingers fly nimbly as she began the intricate needlework that would occupy her much of the day. Most of it she gave away to others. Crippled below the waist from polio contracted after childbirth—and from the many nights she had had to sleep out in the rain under a mango tree because of Nana's cruelty—she bore her pain and misfortune without complaint. Indeed, she was the most cheerful one in the household, the one we all sought out when we needed comfort or advice.

"Have patience, Rabi," she said again. "Patience. We all miss your mommy. But she get a scholarship to study in a university in Benares. You don't know 'bout it, but she set her heart on university before her marriage. Is her karma now—nobody can't stop that."

"You think Mommy go come back *next* year for truth?" I asked.

"Never lose faith in your mommy, Rabi—or in anyone else," replied Ma softly. "Today she intends to come back next year. But if it doesn't happen, then know that there is a cause and accept it patiently." That was difficult advice for me to follow.

Ma had such a gentle manner. Never a harsh word, never a touch of the anger that characterized so many of the other members of the household. She was the peacemaker in family disputes that could sometimes become heated, giving us at times the distinct feeling that Nana's angry spirit was stirring quarrels among his descendants. Ma's sweet disposition was like ointment in a wound.

Not that Nana had only been a quarrelsome man. At times he had seemed the very embodiment of goodness and generosity, loaning money to the poor, even to some of the blacks, who were despised by most Hindus. Nana had been their admired friend and benefactor. Standing on the veranda, he would sometimes toss down handfuls of silver coins in front of the shop below, to the great delight of children and laborers from nearby fields, who would scramble for the money as though it were falling from heaven. Nana had been the first in our part of the island to own a radio—a large, expensive model imported from the United States—and he often generously shared this miracle box. Chairs would be lined up in the large sitting room, neighbors, customers, friends, and relatives would be invited in, and the volume turned up high—like a cinema without a screen. This great honor he dispensed with impartiality to rich and poor alike, all of whom marveled at the spectacular machine.

Nana's evil side, however, seemed to lie just below the surface and would erupt suddenly without warning. Waiting on a customer in the rum shop below, he might leave abruptly in the middle of a transaction, climb the stairs to the living quarters above, grab a heavy leather strap, and, in an explosive rage, begin beating everyone—except me—for no reason that anyone could discover. We accepted it as his karma, something he had to work out from a past life. Hindu mythology is full of stories about demons who administer evil karma. At times it appeared that some of the worst sort had gotten into Nana, turning him in an instant from a Dr. Jekyll to a Mr. Hyde. It was whispered that perhaps the spirits that guarded his wealth had taken possession of his soul, for there seemed something supernatural about his fits of anger and the strength and cunning he exhibited at such times. Yet he was a religious man, too, and every morning and evening did his Hindu prayers and worship, gathering all the children to say the Hindu *bhajans* and to chant the mantras.

Though Nana had taken another wife after Nanee became crippled, there were times when he treated Ma with great kindness. Willing to spend a fortune to find a cure for her, Nana had paid huge sums to pundits who specialized in healing. He took her, too, to obeah men and witch doctors of various kinds, as well as to the large hospital in Port of Spain, and even to a famous Catholic shrine. But neither his money nor the spirits he relied upon were able to effect the slightest improvement. Ma remained paralyzed from her waist down, and only with the greatest effort could she pull herself along the floor.

Tenderly her children would carry Ma about the house—to her chair by the window, into the dining room for meals, into the sitting room when friends and relatives arrived to visit or the pundit came to perform a special *puja*. Most of her waking hours Ma spent sitting in her favorite spot—to which she was carried each morning after her bath—where she could look out past the coconut palms and across the sugarcane fields and mangrove swamps to the bay beyond. Glancing up from her delicate needlework to rest her eyes, she loved to watch the brilliantly colored butterflies and the many varieties of birds flitting from tree to tree or flying in formation high in the sky: kiskadees, black and yellow corn birds, pico plats, and the small blue bird we called *blue jeans* that I was sure had left the footprint on my father's ashes.

While Ma had been in the hospital in Port of Spain, someone had given her a Bible, which she brought home with her. She grew to love that forbidden book, especially the Psalms. When Nana discovered her secretly reading it to her children, he flew into a blind rage.

"I'll teach you never to bring Christian lies into my house!" he had roared in Hindi. Pulling his heavy leather belt off, he had beaten her with all his might, raising large welts on her back and shoulders. Then, picking Ma up in his powerful arms, Nana had carried her out onto the veranda and thrown her down the long flight of stairs. While she lay groaning with pain, he tore the hated book into shreds and threw it into the trash. Somehow she had gotten another Bible, and again he had beaten her savagely and thrown her down the stairs. Faring no better, but for different reasons, Nana's second wife had been driven from the home. But Nanee was too crippled to escape and patiently bore the abuse, accepting it as karma.

That she would read this hated Christian book was a puzzle to me. When a pundit I knew occasionally quoted the Bible, my anger knew no bounds. He was an admirer of Ramakrishna, the famous devotee of Kali and teacher of Vivekenanda, founder of the Vedanta Society. Like Ma, he believed that all religions held some elements of truth and would eventually lead their followers to Brahman. I was already too fanatic a Hindu to agree with that. When I read in the *Bhagavad-Gita* that Lord Krishna had said that all roads led to him, I was greatly displeased. I had to accept it because the *Gita* said it, but consoled myself with the reminder that my religion was the *best* way. Ma's desire to blend her religion with Christianity was the one point of disagreement we had, but we never discussed it.

My Aunt Revati was a very strict Hindu. No Bible reading for her! "Read the *Bhagavad-Gita*, Rabi, over and over," she often exhorted me. I respected her for the religious life she led. She tried to take my mother's place and taught me a great deal from the Vedas, especially from the *Vedanta*, which was her favorite.

I accepted whatever the sacred writings said, although much of it was difficult to understand and seemed contradictory. I had always had a keen awareness that God had always existed and that he had created everything. Yet the Vedas said that there had been a time when nothing had existed—and Brahman had come from nothing. Even Gosine could not reconcile that with Krishna's statement in the *Gita:* "That which is not can never be." It remained an enigma.

The concept of God that I was taught in Hinduism—that a leaf, a bug, a star was God, that Brahman was everything and all was Brahman—did not coincide with the awareness I had of God as not being part of the universe but its Creator, someone other and much greater than myself, not within me as I was taught. Aunt Revati and Gosine both explained that I, like all other humans, was the victim of maya, a misconception about reality that deceived all who were not yet enlightened. I determined to be rid of this ignorance. My father had fought and conquered the illusion of separation from Brahman, and so would I.

After my father's mysterious death, I became a favorite subject for the palm-readers, astrologers, and fortune-tellers who frequently stopped at our house. Our family would hardly make an important decision without consulting an astrologer, so it was vital that my future should be confirmed in the same way. I could never aspire to something that the stars had not ordained. It was therefore encouraging to learn that the lines on my palms and the planets and stars, according to those who interpreted them, all agreed that I would become a great Hindu leader. Yogi, guru, pundit, *sanyasi*, head priest in a temple—the predictions dazzled my young mind.

One especially gifted palmist lived in the small town of Maya about seven miles away. People came from all over the island to consult this attractive daughter of a Brahmin priest about the future. She was particularly popular with the pundits, who consulted her often. Visiting in our home one day, she studied my palm and declared, "You go be a famous Hindu Yogi, marry a beautiful girl before you is twenty-five, have four children, go be so, so rich, and live a long life after be very sick at twenty." Who could ask for more? Truly the gods were smiling upon me!

Another one of the favorite psychics on the island, a young Brahmin who saw cobras sitting beside him when he went into deep meditation, would also often visit in our home. He was in love with my Aunt Revati and hoped to marry her. His predictions about my future as a famous and wealthy pundit were just as glowing. A man with magical powers, who had healed many people of serious infirmities—although he couldn't heal Ma—his predictions were considered to be infallible. With confirmation from so many prognosticators, who could doubt my destiny or that I was very *special*, as Baba Jankhi so often said?

Each time my fortune was told the conviction grew that I was indeed marked with a high Hindu calling. It was no accident that I had been born the son of a famous Yogi venerated by many as an avatar. This was my destiny. As my understanding of karma increased, that, too, became a factor influencing the decision I eventually made. Surely the accumulated effects of my prior lives had made it inevitable that in my present reincarnation I should very soon begin serious study for the Hindu priesthood.

When I made the announcement that I wanted to spend my next summer holiday studying in a temple, no one was happier than my father's half-sister, Phoowa Mohanee. Deeply religious, she often made speeches at large ceremonies—always in Hindi. I respected her wisdom and listened carefully to her advice. Since my father's death, she had showered me with the devotion she had given to him. On her frequent visits she always brought me presents: sweets, clothing, or money. Such gifts to a Brahmin pleased the gods and accumulated good karma for the giver. As soon as she learned of my decision, Phoowa lost no time in coming over to congratulate me.

"Rabi!" she exclaimed, giving me a hug. "You father go be proud of you! What temple you goin' go to?"

"Some place where it have a swami from India," I replied.

"Then the *mandir* in Felicity is jus' the right thing!" exclaimed Ajee, my father's mother, whom Mohanee had brought with her. Ajee had been made blind by a pundit's home remedy, and my father's father, Ajah, had taken another wife. Like so many of the wealthier women who had come from India, Ajee was a walking jewelry store. Both arms, from wrists to elbows, were encased in gold and silver bracelets. Around her neck she wore a solid-gold yoke laden with gold coins, and to one side of her pierced nose clung a golden flower. More gold and silver bracelets circled both ankles above her bare feet. It was quite a contrast she presented to my beloved Nanee, who wore only an occasional bracelet.

"You right. Of course!" agreed Phoowa. "Yeh, the swami who start that temple real good." Her eyes sparkled with enthusiasm. "When you is a small boy, he come from India and you mommy and Revati follow him all 'bout where he go, taking part in all the *pujas*. And he did do a good work in the temple. And the one who there now too, too good. He ain't does make joke at all."

She put her hand on my head and looked into my face. There was a deep pride in her eyes, but something more than pride in her voice—a prophetic authority that sent a shiver through me. "You goin' go be a great Yogi, even greater than anyone think!" she pronounced solemnly. With all my heart I believed her. It was my karma, without a doubt.

It was a singular honor to be accepted to study at Felicity under the famous Brahmacharya in charge of the temple, and I was only ten. Already, however, my reputation had spread throughout our part of the island. Most of the pundits for miles around had known and respected my father and predicted a great future for me, not only because my father had been such a great Hindu but because I, too, had already proven myself by the disciplined religious life I led. Everyone remembered that twelve days after my birth the pundits had arranged a very big *barahi*.

In full obedience to the Vedas and the laws of Manu, I strictly observed the five daily duties of the twice-born: the offering to the gods, to the Seers, to the forefathers, to lower animals, and to humanity, embodied in the daily religious practices which I began at dawn and completed after sunset. Although some religious Hindus would wear leather belts or shoes, I recoiled at the thought of wearing the skin of any creature, especially the cow. It could have been an ancestor, or even a close relative! I made no compromise with my religion, and my reputation as a young pundit-in-the-making spread far beyond my own town.

Rising early each morning, I would immediately repeat the appropriate mantra to Vishnu and offer obeisance inwardly to our family guru. I recited the morning prayer of remembrance most earnestly, resolving thereby to do the day's work under the guidance of Lord Vishnu by affirming that I was one with Brahman: "I am the Lord, in no wise different from Him, the Brahman, suffering from no disabilities such as affliction and anguish. I am existence-knowledge-bliss, ever free. O Lord of the world, all intelligence, the paramount deity, the spouse of Lakshmi, O Vishnu, waking in the early morning I shall comply with the responsibilities of my mundane existence. . . O Lord Hrishikesa, dominating my sensuous entity, with Thee in my heart's cavity, as I am commissioned, so shall I act."

Then came my predawn ceremonial bath, an act of purification that prepared me for the worship that followed. I would then recite the Gayatri mantra, beginning with the names of the three worlds: "*OM*, Bhuh, Bhuvah, Suvah—we meditate upon that adorable effulgence of the resplendent vivifier, Savitar; may he stimulate our intellects." Considered to be the mantra of all mantras, the very essence of the spiritual power a Brahmin gains, I would repeat this ode to the sun derived from the *Rigveda* hundreds of times each day, always in Sanskrit, the language of the gods. The value was in the repetition, the more times the better, and I repeated it rapidly thousands of times as a small child before learning what it meant. More important than understanding the meaning was to correctly articulate the Sanskrit sounds. That alone formed the basis for the efficacy of the mantra. I firmly believed, as do all orthodox Hindus, that the mantra embodied the deity itself, created what it expressed, and that by the proper repetition of the Gayatri mantra and daily worship the sun itself was kept in its proper position.

Next came my morning worship in the prayer room. Solemnly, meditatively, with a sense of awe, I would strike a match and light the *deya*'s cotton ghee-soaked wick, fixing all my attention upon the flickering flame—a god, too. Reverently, yet feeling a sense of my own holiness that I should have such an honor, I would take the sandalwood paste and make the fresh *chanan* mark on the forehead of each god and upon the Shiva lingam. The odor of sandalwood filling the prayer room would send a surge of excitement through me—almost a sexual delight at the thought of my intimacy with my many gods.

Seating myself in lotus position facing east, I would sip water, sprinkle it on myself and around me for ceremonial purification, practice the yoga of breath control, then invoke the deity I was worshiping by *nyasa*, the touching of myself in the forehead, the upper arms, the chest, and the thighs, thereby symbolically placing the deity in my own body. I felt a mystical union with each god I worshiped. Seated before the altar, I would spend an hour in deep meditation, concentrating all attention upon the tip of my nose, until I had lost contact with the world around me and would begin to realize my essential unity with the One Reality underlying the universe. Dismissing the deity with a short water-offering and obeisance, I would go outside, where I would worship the sun for another hour, often staring at it for long periods with both eyes wide open, again repeating the Gayatri mantra hundreds of times, believing, as I had been taught, that it had the power of saving the soul fully devoted to it. I loved my religion. And as I worshiped my father's memory, I knew that he must be pleased.

Although inwardly I was filled with the excitement of eager anticipation, there was a sadness in my heart, too, that morning when Uncle Kumar was to drive me and my little suitcase in the large yellow convertible—the only one of its kind on the island—to the temple in Felicity. I would miss my dear friend Gosine, who seemed to grow older by the day. Following the familiar path out through the gate and across a narrow lane, I found him sitting in the sun softly repeating his morning mantras. Hearing my approach, he interrupted his worship to greet me.

"So you go leave today," he said after we had solemnly bowed to each other. "I was thinkin' of you early when I wake up this mornin', and then my mind turn to your Ajah. That is a good, good sign! Don't mind he drink so much in his last days, but 'e was a master pundit. Good sign, man! I ain't think of him for a long time."

"I wish he was still livin'," I said wistfully. "They say he was high-quality Indian." I remembered him so well—tall, fair skin, gray eyes, almost like a white man but every inch a Brahmin.

"Give the man the credit he deserve," said Gosine solemnly, as though he were a judge carefully weighing evidence. "He didn't *have* to leave India and come out quite here . . . when it hardly had any pundits. I 'member it then.

But he come and he do a master job, and he plenty help we Indians. The Indian people in my generation make good use o' him. And he make good use of the *dakshina*, too," he added with a mischievous twinkle in his eye.

"You knew him then?" Of course I knew the answer to that question, but it would have been impolite not to ask.

"If I *know* him? You askin' old Gosine *that?* People use to give him ton load of all kind of things. He use to have piles and piles of ghee and butter and rice and flour. And so he collectin' dhotis for so. But I sure he was doin' better in India."

Lowering his voice, he adopted a confidential, almost secretive tone and leaned closer to me.

"We was *real-real* friends. He was *rich*, man—not like at the end when rum finish him off. I never been nothin' but poor. That is my karma. But still he good friend to Gosine. Good Hindu, great pundit. Make a real *puja*, no shortcut na. Is a real mystery why he get so unhappy, why he start drinkin' so much. An' jus' imagine, today I thinkin' of 'im—'e jus' come in m'head like that. Good-good sign!" He patted my shoulder. "Very fav'able time you goin' to Felicity *mandir*. You go be great pundit, great Yogi! *Bhai*, I tellin' you, you is you father true-true son!"

My eyes glistened with tears as I waved from the car when it pulled out onto the main road. Ma had been carried to a front window and was waving good-bye. My cousins were jumping up and down in front of the shop downstairs shouting their farewells. It wasn't easy to leave them all behind, but I knew that my decision was the right one. If only my father were alive, I thought. He would be pleased. Aunt Revati would write to my mother to give her the news. I felt good inside, proud to be following in my father's footsteps. Gosine's words rang in my ear, and I felt a growing excitement. My karma was good and destiny was calling.

FOUR

Pundit Ji

The *mandir* in Felicity, dedicated to Vishnu, spouse of
Lakshmi, seemed at a glance to be much like other small-town
temples in Trinidad. Its appearance, with badly smudged
whitewashed walls, packed dirt floor, and galvanized tin
roof, with banners and shrines in the small courtyard, was
less ostentatious than the temples in the larger cities and
lacked the high walls and lofty, ornately carved entrance of
the older structures in India. Such outward embellishments
are important to the Hindu mind. But the inner sanctuary is
really the heart of the temple, a picture of the heart of man,
where the deity, represented by the image, resides. The small
courtyard was dominated by a large image of Vishnu standing guard in front of the main doorway, through which one
could see, at the far end of the public sanctuary, the holy
place sealed off by a low railing.

When I arrived in the courtyard, a businessman, his shoes
having been left at the outer gate, his briefcase on the ground
beside him, lay prostrate in worship before the large Shiva
lingam. Several other worshipers were perambulating rapidly
around a shrine containing favorite gods just inside the low
wall surrounding the courtyard. Such efforts earned the favor of the deities.

In spite of its plain appearance, Felicity's temple had a
reputation as one of the best in the island, for its head priest
was a brilliant and highly respected young Brahmin thor-

oughly learned in Hinduism. Still only in his middle twenties, very handsome, with an athletic physique and magnetic personality, this young swami was every Brahmin's ideal. He was a Brahmacharya, having taken the vow of celibacy. I considered it a great privilege to be able to study under such a worthy Hindu. He seemed equally pleased to have me there.

The room I shared with a young man in his late teens was very plain, with bare walls and floors and an open doorway that allowed no privacy. Each of us had an ancient, extremely narrow, low bed of bare wooden planks. Although exceptionally religious for his age, my roommate was not a Brahmin and therefore could not participate in the training I received.

Our day began very early. During the last eighth of the night, the auspicious lamp ceremony would be performed to awaken Vishnu, the temple deity. After the idol had been bathed and worshiped, we would all gather at about five thirty to hear the Vedas read aloud in Hindi; then we would spend two or three hours in meditation. The first mantra assigned to me was *Hari OM Tat Sat*. The Brahmacharya would always begin his meditation with the repetition of the single word, *OM*. The highest vibration and the most difficult to pronounce, like all mantras *OM* must be taught by a guru. In the Vedas it is said that

> on the lotus . . . Brahma began to think: "By what single syllable may I be able to enjoy all desires, all worlds . . . gods . . . Vedas . . . rewards . . . ?" He saw this *OM* . . . all-pervading, omnipresent . . . the Brahman's own symbolic syllable. . . . With it he enjoyed all the desires of all worlds, all gods, all Vedas . . . all rewards, all beings. . . . Therefore the Brahmin who, desiring whatever he wants, fasts three nights, sits on sacred grass facing east, and repeats this imperishable *OM*, for him all objects are realized and all acts are successful.

Nothing was more important than our daily transcendental meditation, the heart of Yoga, which Krishna advocated as the surest way to eternal Bliss. But it could also be dangerous. Frightening psychic experiences awaited the unwary meditator, similar to a bad trip on drugs. Demons described in the Vedas had been known to take possession of some Yogis. *Kundalini* power, said to be coiled like a serpent at the base of the spine, could produce ecstatic experiences when released in deep meditation—or, if not properly controlled, it could do great mental and even bodily harm. The line between ecstasy and horror was very fine. For that reason we initiates were closely supervised by the Brahmacharya and his assistant.

During the daily meditation I began to have visions of psychedelic colors, heard unearthly music, and even visited exotic planets where the gods conversed with me, encouraging me to attain even higher states of consciousness. Sometimes in my trance I encountered the same horrible demonic creatures that are depicted by the images in Hindu, Buddhist, Shinto, and other religious temples. It was a frightful experience, but the Brahmacharya explained that it was normal and urged me to pursue the quest for Self-realization. At times I experienced a sense of mystical unity with the universe. I *was* the universe, Lord of all, omnipotent, omnipresent. My instructors were excited at this. I was obviously a chosen vessel, destined for early success in the search for union with Brahman. The Forces that had guided my father were now guiding me.

Already a very small eater, I learned even more about self-denial during my three months of training at the temple. My one daily meal I ate with a wealthy Hindu family that operated an adjacent dairy. They were pleased to have a Brahmin in their home for the noon meal. Feeding a Brahmin is guaranteed to add good karma. In turn I was excited to have a whole herd of cows to worship.

Much to my surprise, I discovered that those who are practicing self-denial in some areas of life can at the same time indulge themselves in other ways. One young man of about thirty, in training to become a holy man, seemed to me to take far too many pains with his personal appearance, spending much time arranging his long dark hair and adjusting his clothing. The one part of his appearance that he neglected was his paunch, which grew steadily from his constant over-eating. It shocked me to learn that he was carrying on affairs with several of the girls who frequented the temple.

"Hey, man, what you think 'bout Shama? Nice, yeh?" he asked me one day. Shama was about twelve, with a pretty face and long jet-black wavy hair—one of a number of girls who hung around the temple constantly but spent little time in serious worship. "She in love with you! Here, take this cake she make for you."

I felt my face turn red. "I'm not in love with her—or any of 'em!" I retorted righteously and indignantly.

Unperturbed, he winked and gave me a sly grin. "It have a good-good place to get alone with her—and nobody go know it!"

My cheeks were burning now. "Stop! I ain't go talk 'bout such things!"

"You ain't fool me. I see you lookin' at the girls."

"It ain't true! I never go get married. I goin' be jus' like the Brahmacharya!"

He threw back his head and laughed. "You think *he* a Brahmacharya? Now hear me, I go tell you. . . ." There were footsteps in the hallway, and he clamped his mouth shut. Trying to hold in my anger, I marched from the room and almost ran into the Brahmacharya just outside the door. I was embarrassed that he might think I had been listening to gossip about him, but apparently he hadn't heard a word.

"You look like you're in a hurry," he said with a smile, and continued in the direction of his own room.

A few days later, while walking quietly through the sleeping quarters after the lamp ceremony when the deity had been put to rest for the night, I heard one of the young initiates sobbing in his room. Curious, I paused just outside his door, then froze at the sound of the Brahmacharya's voice hissing in suppressed anger. "You are the one talking about me outside! Don't try to deny it!" Then, in a smoother tone, "Of course, girls are always in *every* temple. They have a right to be here like anyone else. And I have a right to spend as much time with any of them as I please. Any more of your stories and you'll have to leave here!"

I couldn't imagine what stories had been told. Lies, no doubt. My sympathy and loyalty were with the swami. Never would I doubt his holiness. Of course it was normal for girls and women to hang around like they did at other temples. Thereafter I began to notice, however, that a slender girl in her late twenties—let's call her Parabathi—was obviously in love with the Brahmacharya. Reluctantly I had to admit also that he treated her with the tenderness of a lover, although in a guarded way when anyone was watching. It seemed strange that I had not noticed this before. An exceptionally beautiful girl, Parabathi spent a great deal of time with him alone in his room—supposedly preparing and serving food that she brought for him each day, but it hardly seemed possible that it could take so long. Although my young mind didn't fully understand, his conduct hardly seemed appropriate for one who had vowed never to marry. Having admired this brilliant young Brahmin, I was now badly disillusioned and troubled.

One day I overheard several regular worshipers discussing the affair in Hindi as they squatted in a tight group on the packed earth of the courtyard. "This is a private matter—we better not meddle in it," said one handsome man in his forties.

An older, white-haired man with long beard, whom I had seen often at the temple, nodded gravely. "Of course it's karma. They have something from their last life to work out together." There were sounds of assent and heads nodded in agreement. It made me feel better.

My days were too full to give much thought to the Brahmacharya's lapses. Karma would make it all work out in the end. I could not doubt that. Even a neighbor's dog that I had observed for years seemed to be living proof of karma and reincarnation. Affectionately named Yogi, this lean black hound had a flowing white beard. A strict vegetarian, Yogi steadfastly refused to touch not only bones and meat but even eggs. Though he had a Muslim master, he was clearly of Hindu persuasion and faithfully attended all the big religious ceremonies. Surely he was accumulating good karma now, having learned a hard lesson in a previous life. The fact that he often became loud and quarrelsome with the other dogs convinced me that he was the reincarnation of a Yogi who had fallen into bad karma. In fact, I had known a pundit who acted exactly like Yogi. It angered me that so many Hindus mistreated dogs. How could they believe in reincarnation and treat any animal as less than human? When we discovered that Yogi came to the ceremonies because he loved the food served afterward, it only confirmed my belief in reincarnation. I knew a number of pundits who were no less fond of these same delicacies, and many Hindus obviously enjoyed the food much more than the religious ritual.

When I returned home at the end of that summer, I discovered that my training in the temple had elevated me considerably in the eyes of religious Hindus. Walking through town on my way to school that fall, I was the center of worshipful attention.

"Sita-Ram, Pundit Ji," people called out, hurrying over to bow low before me. I loved it. Especially gratifying was the recognition I was given by the pundits.

Often when I passed his home on the way to school, Pundit Bhajan—a large bulky man with long black hair knotted behind—would be out in his yard picking flowers for his day's *pujas*, preparing to leave on his rounds. Seeing me approach he would clasp his hands together in front of him, bow low and call out, "Pundit Maharaj, *namahste Ji*."

"*Namahste Ji*, Pundit Bhajan," I would reply solemnly, feeling good inside.

Although I did not yet consider myself to have fully

achieved Self-realization, I felt that I was very close to *jivan-mukti*, the highest ideal for man set forth in the *Bhagavad-Gita*. To attain this deliverance from original ignorance while still in the body would assure me that I would never be reincarnated again, but would be reunited with Brahman, my true Self, forever. I was now convinced that this was the state my father had reached, and I sought the same liberation from the illusion of individual existence. I was the One and Only Brahman, pure existence-consciousness-bliss; so it was to be expected that others, recognizing the degree to which I had realized this loftiest ideal, should bow down and worship me.

Indeed, seated before a mirror I worshiped myself. And why not? *I was God*. Krishna, in the precious and beautiful *Bhagavad-Gita*, had promised this divine knowledge to the one who practiced Yoga. This was the nectar for the meditators to drink. It wasn't a question of becoming God but of simply realizing who I really was and had been all of the time. Walking the streets I felt that I really was the Lord of the universe and my creatures were bowing before me.

Though it was not easy to accept worship graciously, I gradually learned how to appear humble without compromising my deity. It was only necessary to remember that all men were of the same Essence—except, of course, those who were not among the four Hindu castes. It became my great ambition to teach qualified Hindus the truth about their essential deity, to liberate them from the chains of ignorance. I would become a guru, for the guru is a teacher, and without his help the Hindu has no hope for deliverance from the wheel of reincarnation.

One of the gurus most popular in Trinidad at that time was His Holiness Swami Sivananda. We received his bulletins regularly from India, describing the large *pujas* and happenings at his temple, advertising his books—one of which was entitled *My God Sivananda*—explaining his teachings and containing testimonial letters from his many followers. There were always several of his pictures included to enable us better to worship him. A large photograph of Sivananda had a prominent place on our altar, always with a fresh *chanan* mark on the forehead. It was a great thrill for the family when we received a letter from my mother describing her visit to Sivananda's ashram. She had been overcome by his Divine presence and assured us that he was a very holy man, a Self-realized Master. I determined to become just like him. After his sudden death from cancer, we worshiped him as one of the Ascended Masters in the long line of gurus stretching back to the days of the Rishis.

In spite of my growing reputation for piety and the worshipful attention I received, there was still much of the small boy in me. The anticipation of presents and stockings filled by Santa Claus at Christmas still excited me as much as ever. Being a British colony, Trinidad was alive for weeks with the strains of "Jingle Bells," "Deck the Halls with Boughs of Holly," and other Christmas songs. The Hindu and Buddhist merchants had no qualms about joining in the festivities. It meant extra profits, and one's religious convictions must not interfere with anything so important as that. Even the Muslims joined the annual celebration. Santa Claus was everyone's patron saint during that time of the year, the most beloved of all gods for the moment.

We children were required to go to bed early on Christmas eve, while the grown-ups went from house to house drinking rum and setting off firecrackers. The older children would pound on large pans and drums. It was a noisy time to expect children to fall asleep, but we knew that Santa Claus would not land his reindeer and deliver our presents so long as a "creature was stirring." On this Christmas eve, however, I was determined to catch a glimpse of Santa even if I had to stay awake all night. I made careful preparations to be sure he wouldn't know I was watching.

"Hey! Why for you doin' that?" asked Ananda, one of my younger cousins, who shared a large double bed for a time with me after my mother left for India. With a pair of Nanee's scissors, I was cutting two small peepholes in the sheet. We seldom used blankets in that tropical climate, but a sheet was always necessary if only as protection from the mosquitoes.

"Shh!" was the only reply I would give him. "Shh!"

"Why you ain't go t'sleep?" he insisted, feeling the bed shake as I tried to maneuver into a comfortable position with the sheet covering me and my eyes peering out from those two small holes.

"Shh! You suppose to be sleepin'!"

"An' you too."

"Nobody can't sleep with all the noise you makin'."

"You makin' the noise. Stop wigglin'."

"Shh!"

Eventually Ananda began to snore quietly. I struggled to stay awake, concentrating all my attention on the window through which Santa made his annual entry into our room. On Christmas morning the one apple I had all year, along with some tasty nuts, would be in my stocking at the foot of the bed, and this time I was going to see Santa fill it. Time dragged ever so slowly. It seemed to me that I couldn't stay awake another minute, when I heard a noise in the room. It wasn't coming from the direction of the window, however, but from behind me! Startled, I almost lurched around, then caught myself and cautiously twisted my head, keeping the two holes in front of my eyes. Dimly I could see my Uncle Kumar tiptoeing to the foot of our bed, arms loaded. Laying presents down, he dipped nuts and two apples out of a large bag and filled our stockings. Then he left quietly after one last glance at the two motionless figures in the bed, certain his work had gone undetected.

Nearly bursting with my discovery, I had to wait until after breakfast to break the startling news when I got alone with Krishna and Shanti, my two oldest cousins.

"It ain't have no Santa Claus!" I announced dramatically.

"What?" exclaimed Shanti, her eyes wide with disbelief.

"It ain't have no Santa," I repeated, " 'less you want to call Uncle Kumar Santa Claus."

"You makin' joke or what?" demanded Krishna with the superior tone of one who is older and wiser. "Where you think those presents come from? If you want to know, Santa bring them quite from the North Pole!"

"No, it ain't Santa who bring them at all!" I declared in an all-knowing tone. "It's Uncle Kumar—he is who Santa is!"

"Why you foolin' us for!" exclaimed Shanti, almost ready to cry, disillusionment spreading across her face.

"I played a good trick on 'im las' night . . . and I *see* 'im with my own two eyes wide-wide open!"

"See *who?*"

"Uncle Kumar, fillin' stockin's! Like I tryin' t'tell you."

The devastating news spread swiftly among the children in our household, then around the neighborhood. Waxing philosophical, I decided that it wasn't so surprising after all. Of course the Christian gods were just myths, not real like the gods we Hindus worshiped, who could sometimes be seen—in visions during meditation, and in spirit form, too. We knew nothing of the careful verification of such appearances by parapsychologists and other scientific researchers, nor that such phenomena followed men as famous and unemotional as Dr. Carl Jung. We only knew what we experienced, and it was very real.

"Ai! Rev! Ai! Look there!"

I sat up in bed and rubbed my eyes, frightened, trying to see in the darkness. Hurried footsteps passed outside my bedroom. There were muffled excited voices, as Nanee continued to scream for Aunt Revati in Hindi.

When lights began to go on in the house, I found courage to creep out from under the sheet and run toward Nanee's bedroom, where voices were joined in a loud and excited babble.

"I just saw . . I just saw Nana!" Ma was saying in a frightened voice in Hindi when I ran into her room. Half of the household was gathered around her bed, listening intently. "It was Nana, I'm sure . . . but he didn't have any head!" Trembling and pale Ma pointed toward the window. "I woke up feeling something strange . . . and there he was! I could see him in the moonlight shining through the window."

"Sure you weren't dreaming?" asked Aunt Revati.

"*Nehi!* I was wide awake. He started coming toward me, and that's when I screamed. I don't know how I yelled so loud."

"You can't say it was for *sure* you Nana's spirit," said Gosine thoughtfully later that morning when we talked it over together in front of his hut. "It have plenty spirit around. All over de place."

"But my Nanee say is Nana who she see!"

"It ain't so easy," insisted Gosine. He stroked his chin several times, then looked at me out of the corner of his eye. "Some pundit and them does use spirit. Ain't we have one jus' down de road—you know who I mean. Them spirit does do what he tell them to do. Sometime bad things, sometime good things."

"You mean I go have to use them spirit too as a pundit?"

Gosine just shrugged and looked away. "I ain't say *all* of 'em does do it. Some of 'em could work without skull."

"How he does get the spirit and them to work for him?"

"*Bhai*, ev'ry people know he goin' in de cemet'ry an' dig up somebody skull. Once you got that skull, you can get the person spirit to work for you."

"You mean somebody got Nana's skull? And that is why it ain't have no head on that . . that *thing* what she see? But his grave have a watchman."

Gosine looked uncomfortable. He shrugged again and struggled to his feet, glancing apprehensively at the sky. Thunderheads were piling up over the Gulf. "I think we goin' go get some rain soon." Shaking his head, he turned to go into his hut. "I don't play with this spirit thing," he said, as he ducked under the low doorway. "Is a hell of a thing."

Lightning streaked the sky and the rain came down in sheets as I ran toward the house. The rumble of thunder was frightening. Perhaps the gods were angry.

FIVE

Young Guru

Through the open windows the booming sound of drums drifted into the classroom, causing a restless stir among the students. Huge drums that could be heard for miles, they were being tuned and warmed up for that evening's Ramleela festival in Dow Village where the school was located about a mile from my home. The week-long pageant depicted the entire epic of the *Ramayana*. I had been daydreaming of India, trying to imagine the village a pundit had told me I'd lived in during my previous life. Now the rhythmic beat of the drums gave my imagination fresh stimulus. I saw myself as Rama, then as Hanuman, the monkey god, fighting against the evil Ravana. By contrast school seemed so dull. Why was I, Lord of the universe, one with Brahman and of his essence, suffering through another lesson in English grammar? I hardly heard a word the teacher was saying.

I was only eleven and already many people were bowing before me, laying gifts of money, cotton cloth, and other treasures at my feet and hanging garlands of flowers around my neck at religious ceremonies. Should I quit school and go back to the temple, as my mother had done, for more intensive religious training? Nanee and Aunt Revati both advised against it, but the temptation was strong, especially on hot afternoons like this in a stifling classroom. My long hours of meditation and other religious practices left little time or energy for school.

When the last bell sounded, I ran joyfully from the classroom. Accompanied by several admirers, I ran toward the market square, eager to be among the first to reach the site of the festivities. The booming of drums grew louder as we hurried on.

"I want you to be my guru, Rabi!" The earnest declaration came from Ramjit, whose parents were of the Kshatriya caste, like Nana had been. His father was a foreman in the cane fields and wore the khaki cork hat of an overseer with pride.

"And mine!" added Mohan, a very religious boy who regularly attended the *sandhya* classes where I helped to instruct young Hindus in their religious duties. Mohan's father was a Vaisya and a wealthy wholesaler of sugar from the nearby factory where my father had worked as an engineer before his marriage.

I smiled, pleased with their eagerness. "I can't talk 'bout it an' run so fast," I said between deep breaths. My chest had been paining me lately, and I knew it was due to my heavy smoking. "We go talk 'bout it when we get there," I added breathlessly. Already in my town there were many who looked to me for spiritual help. One day I would be the guru for thousands.

The narrow, rutted streets of Dow Village—lined with the cane workers' small mud huts and dirt-floored wooden shacks—were already crowded. We hurried past the brightly decorated shops to the large open field in the center of the village. Here each evening the dramatization of a portion of the *Ramayana* was being enacted. Vendors, calling out their wares to the noisy, jostling crowd, were selling drinks and sweets and spicy foods from temporary booths, pushcarts, and bicycle trays—or from large bowls and trays spread on the ground and filled with *bara* and mango chutney, curry *channa*, fried *channa*, and various Indian sweets like *jilabhi*. Here and there a fortune-teller or palm-reader squatted on the edge of the crowd, laying out cards or diagrams of the hand, attracting clusters of customers and the curious around them.

I had plenty of spending money. In a locked cupboard

at home I kept the accumulating cache of money from the gifts being laid at my feet by worshipers. Some pundits were among the wealthiest of Hindus, and already I was learning how quickly and effortlessly the money piled up. Poorer people of lower castes were often the largest source of a pundit's income. One pundit I knew specialized in good-luck *pujas* for winning lotteries and sweepstakes and accumulating wealth. The poor who regularly paid his fees remained poor, while he grew wealthy and could always point to himself as proof that his magical powers worked.

I was in the very front row of spectators that evening when the pundit blew a long deep blast on the conch and pronounced his blessing to signal the start of the pageant. The opposing armies, played by men of high caste, already lined up impressively in colorful costumes at either end of the field, now began their dancing approach toward each other in time with the deep booming of the drums. Evil Ravana had stolen Rama's wife, Sita, who was played by a young man dressed up in a brightly colored sari because no women were allowed to participate. Hanuman, the monkey king and real hero of the story, had discovered where Sita was being held captive. Rama and his brothers and supporters, joined by Hanuman and his monkey army, were pitted against the power of Ravana and his evil cohorts. What an imposing and colorful spectacle it was as they fought back and forth to the accompaniment of the huge *tassas*'s martial beat and the shrill shouts of the spectators! I loved every minute of it and easily forgot that at school I fancied myself to be a young Mahatma Gandhi, keeping peace between the Hindus and Muslims who otherwise were prone to engage in name-calling and fistfights. "Nonviolence is the duty of all castes!" I often exhorted the Hindu boys, and generally they would obey me as their spiritual leader. But at the Ram-leela festival I—and hundreds of other vegetarians for nonviolence—exulted in the exploits of Hanuman and Rama on the battlefield, and the more violent the participants could make it appear the better we liked it.

My mother had carefully taught me the epic's spiritual message: that Rama represented good and Ravana evil. The battle they fought depicted the constant conflict between good and evil within the heart of every man. In the festive atmosphere and under the spell of those drums I could forget for a few moments, but when I returned home late that night, accompanied by Shanti, Sandra, Ananda, and Amar, I had to face once again the struggle between good and evil that was raging in my own heart. Why should I sense this conflict between good and evil when all was One? It puzzled me. Brahman was the only reality. All else was illusion. Then surely the evil Ravana was Brahman also, just as Rama, the avatar, was Brahman. And so was I. In my Yogic trances I was the Lord of the universe, with no problems, no unrest, no uncertainty. The trick was to retain this transcendent consciousness when I was not meditating. Perhaps the only hope was to do as my father had done—withdraw entirely from this world of illusion. But how then could I be a guru and teach others?

Aunt Revati's youngest child, Amar, was one of my best pupils. Only five, he reminded me of myself at that age, which may have been why I was so fond of him. Already he was doing his own *puja*, offering water to the sun each morning, and showing signs of unusual religious zeal. I was training him in meditation, teaching him special mantras, and in turn he held me in the highest esteem.

"You ain't lookin' so well these days, Rabi! I so worried 'bout your health," Ma told me solemnly the next morning when I sat down to visit with her just before leaving for school. "You look so pale, and you coughin' so much!"

"Nothin' wrong with me, Ma," I insisted. "I am okay—" Here I was taken by a sudden fit of coughing that doubled me over.

"Rabi! Your Uncle Kumar will have to take you to a doctor before he go to England!"

"Nothin' wrong, Ma," I managed to say, gasping for

breath. How my chest ached, especially around my heart! "I will be all right."

"You been coughin' so much for weeks now! I does hear you every night."

"It ain't nothin' at all. Don't worry, Ma. Ev'rybody coughs. How *you* feelin' today?" I wanted to change the subject, fearful that Nanee might suspect the truth. I had been smoking heavily in secret for months—certain that Nanee and my aunts and uncles would insist that I was still too young—and the habit was now beyond my power to break. I often thought how strange it was that I was so strict about my vegetarianism—I wouldn't buy cheese in a store if it had been cut with a knife that had been used on meat—and yet I couldn't stop smoking, even though I knew it was ruining my lungs. Out in the fields alone I chain-smoked one cigarette after another, inhaling deeply with every puff. And worst of all, because I didn't want anyone to know of my secret habit, I had to *steal* the cigarettes, even though I had plenty of money . . . and that troubled my conscience deeply. Truly the battle between Ravana and Rama was raging within my own soul, and I seemed helpless to affect the outcome. Ravana was winning, in spite of my fervent prayers to Hanuman.

For the first time, as I walked to school that day, I felt a hollowness inside when I received the usual greeting, "Sita-Ram, Pundit Ji," from admirers. It wasn't so much my conversation with Ma, knowing I had lied to her, that bothered me. I was preoccupied with a distressing experience that had happened earlier that morning.

Holding a small brass cup, or lota, of holy water in one hand for a purification offering, I had just placed a fresh hibiscus bloom on our cow's head, which I did every morning, and was bowing in worship . . . when suddenly, with a warning snort, the big black creature lowered her head and charged. I jumped back, barely avoiding a tossing horn, then turned to run, dropping the lota and prayer beads. My god was chasing me! Fortunately for me, I hadn't yet untied the cow. Her rope pulled her up short just as I thought her horns were going to impale me. Shaken and breathless, I looked from the trampled lota and beads and angrily pawing hoofs to those big brown eyes staring at me with intense hatred. *Attacked by my god!* And I had worshiped her faithfully for an hour each day for years!

On my way to school, two hours after this had happened, I was still shaking inside—no longer with fright, but with bewildered grief. *Why?* Though Shiva and Kali and so many of the other gods often frightened me, the cow was one god I had always adored. Grazing and caring for her was the one chore I had delighted in. I had always treated the cow, and all other animals, with the utmost kindness. Then *why* should this god attack *me?* It was a question that would continue to haunt me in the days ahead. Even Gosine couldn't settle this one.

SIX

Shiva and I

In the early thirties, at considerable expense, Nana had sat
for a portrait with the island's best photographer, who had
found Nana a difficult man to please and had charged him
accordingly. The photograph finally settled upon, showing
Nana in a patriarchal pose with a piercing gaze, had been
matched to a large and expensive gilt frame and hung in the
living room in a dominant position. Entering that room from
any direction—and one had to pass through it to go anywhere
in the house—one immediately was confronted by Nana's
stare. The eyes seemed to follow us wherever we walked, as
though Nana's spirit was looking out of them to observe
what went on after his death in the house he had built with
that money from the unknown source. I was afraid to look
at those eyes. They haunted me.

I felt the same way about Shiva, the god I feared the
most and therefore worshiped the most in order to appease
him. But there was no appeasing Nana's spirit. It continued
to frighten us with wild running or stomping footsteps, a
disagreeable odor that accompanied them and lingered on,
and objects that would be thrown out of cupboards or
shoved from tables, sometimes before our wondering eyes.

In spite of my efforts to appease Shiva, I had a growing
sense of his displeasure. Try as I might with mantras and ritual
and worship, I could find no peace in my relationship with
this fearsome god known as the Destroyer. Often in deep
meditation I found myself on another world alone with Shiva,

and his manner was always threatening. As I ran through my Aunt Sumintra's yard one day a nail had pierced my bare foot. Lying in bed, feverish with the infection, I had not been able to shake the distinct impression that Shiva had placed the large nail there and guided my foot onto it. I tried to dismiss that feeling as mere superstition, but when I mentioned it to my cousin Krishna a knowing look came into his eyes. He shared with me that he, too, had the same impression that Shiva was attacking him. One night while studying late he had been slapped by invisible hands until he'd fallen down, and the next morning the marks were still on his face for us all to see. Another night invisible hands had choked him on his bed, and again he had felt that it was Shiva. I had experienced several other attacks that I felt were from Shiva, but neither Krishna nor I could understand why these things were happening to us. Gosine was no help. He didn't like to talk about such things—and I knew why.

These mysterious physical attacks and the continued haunting of the house by Nana's spirit had a cumulative unnerving effect upon all of us. Beneath the surface there was a tension that could not help but affect personal relationships. This was especially the case with myself and Aunt Revati. Although we had once been so close, we could hardly get along at all anymore, and sometimes even quarreled in the middle of a family *puja*. My mother had been in India now for about six years, and I was tired of being treated like one of my aunt's children. With a round face and hearty laugh, she was a changeable person, given to extreme moods—feeding her children sweets one moment and spanking them the next. At times I suspected that underneath the buoyant personality that attracted a steady stream of friends to our house she was a very unhappy person—and with good reason, after all she had suffered at the hands of her estranged husband. I speculated that in her last life she had been a wifebeater, and now in this life karma had repaid her with the same fate.

Aunt Revati had been the religious leader in the household when I was younger, but now she had to submit to my spiritual authority. This created increasing tension between us, and I suspected that more than a little jealousy had developed as I grew older. The long hours she spent each day in the prayer room doing her *puja*, in meditation, and in worshiping the sun and the cow were more than enough to cause her to fall behind in her household responsibilities. This made her feel harassed, and she often took her irritability out on the rest of us—especially on me. In turn, I resented her attempts to involve me in household chores that were beneath my lofty calling. It was not fitting for me to take time from my religious observances for menial duties that others could perform. The only thing I willingly did was graze the cow—caring for this holiest of creatures was beneficial to one's karma—but since it had attacked me, I had lost my enthusiasm even for that job. My cow worship, too, had stopped.

It troubled me deeply to see how the state of blissful peace I had reached in meditation could so easily be destroyed by a scolding from my aunt accusing me of laziness or of failing to do my fair share around the house. Normally a peaceful person, at such times my temper would flare and I would use harsh language in defending myself. Occasionally I almost suspected that Nana's angry spirit took temporary possession of me. There were times when I acted just like him, beating one of the concrete pillars supporting the veranda with the long whiplike branch of a lash plant until I stood exhausted, staring at the crisscross pattern I had made on the rough cement, wondering what had gotten into me. Once I grabbed Nana's old leather strap which he had so often beaten the family with, and lashed it repeatedly across the backs of several of my younger girl cousins, then retreated in confusion and shame. The scene was so poignantly reminiscent of Nana's wild rages. After such episodes, the eyes in Nana's portrait seemed to laugh at me—if I made the mistake of glancing at them—as though they knew some secret. I would shudder and quickly turn away, but the memory stayed with me. Surely he was haunting us, not only by the sound of his footsteps, but through me as well. Why should *I*, the most religious one in the household, be the vehicle for his spirit to continue to abuse the family long after his death? It was a question I couldn't face because it seemed to involve everything I believed in.

Trying to forget these incidents, I lived for the religious ceremonies—public ones in the temple or private ones in our own home or those of others, where friends and relatives would crowd in. There I would be the center of attention, admired by all. I loved to move through the audience, sprinkling holy water on worshipers or marking foreheads with the sacred white sandalwood paste, or gathering the offering until the brass plate I carried was piled high with blue, red, and green bank notes of different denominations looking like a huge bouquet of money blooms. Best of all, I loved to sit next to the altar and beside the officiating pundit, the object of admiring eyes. How I enjoyed, too, the deep fragrance of the floral garlands hanging around my neck on these occasions! And the worshipers, after the ceremony, bowing low before me to leave their offerings at my feet!

Although the peace I experienced in meditation so easily deserted me, the occult forces that my practice of Yoga cultivated and aroused lingered on and began to manifest themselves in public. Knowing that without these displays of the supernatural my following could never be very great, I welcomed this growing spiritual power. Often those who bowed before me would sense a brightness and experience an inner illumination when I touched them on the forehead in bestowal of my blessing. Only thirteen, and already I was administering the "Shakti pat" famous among gurus, a true mark of the authenticity of my calling! Shakti is one of the names given to Kali, Shiva's murderous, blood-drinking consort, the mother goddess of power who dispenses the primal force flowing at the heart of the universe. How it excited me to become a channel of her power!

Often while I was in deep meditation the gods became

visible and talked with me. At times I seemed to be transported by astral projection to distant planets or to worlds in other dimensions. It would be years before I would learn that such experiences were being duplicated in laboratories under the watchful eyes of parapsychologists through the use of hypnosis and LSD. In my Yogic trances most often I would be alone with Shiva the Destroyer, sitting fearfully at his feet, the huge cobra coiled about his neck staring at me, hissing and darting out its tongue threateningly. Sometimes I wondered why none of the gods I ever encountered seemed kind and gentle and loving. But at least they were real—I had no doubt of that—and not mere myths like the Christian god Santa Claus.

What a happy day it was for me when my Uncle Deonarine, Nana's eldest son, returned at last from England, having graduated with honors from London University! When Uncle Kumar had moved to London a few months earlier, Aunt Revati's matriarchal and authoritarian grip on the household had tightened. Now, with Deonarine's return, we would have a *man* at the head of the family again. Deonarine had been the nearest thing to a real father I had ever known. Perhaps his return would encourage my mother to return, too. She still wrote every two or three months, but there was no more mention of coming back "next year."

One day shortly after his return Uncle Deonarine took me quietly aside. "I've just bought a new car, Rabi, and I want you to bless it," he said earnestly. "I won't drive it anywhere without your blessing!"

I beamed. And to think I had been afraid that he would come back from London having abandoned Hinduism! Deonarine had shown little interest in religion for years, but now he seemed to be a strong Hindu at last. "Just wait a moment," I said, trying to use proper English. "I'm going to get some things. I'll be right back."

I gave that car a thorough blessing, chasing every evil

spirit away and calling down the protection of the most powerful gods upon it. Uncle Deonarine even paid me a handsome fee, although I protested that it wasn't necessary. In the end I consented, not wishing to rob him of the great benefit that accrues to those giving gifts to Brahmins.

"You've got to go on to high school, Rabi!" Deonarine insisted one morning when he and I were visiting with Ma. I was about to graduate from the school in Dow Village and had been talking about going back to the temple at Felicity, or perhaps even to the large one in Port of Spain.

"Rabi, you've *got* to have a higher education," he continued earnestly, while Ma nodded her head emphatically. "I mean university too. It's important for communicating ideas. No matter how enlightened you are yourself, how can you be a good teacher unless you can explain things clearly to others. As well as a thorough knowledge of the Vedas, you need a *general* education too!"

"You may be right," I conceded reluctantly, hanging my head in disappointment. I had been looking forward to being done with the agony of school, but there was no denying the logic of what he said. I decided to take the entrance exam for the same high school that my cousin Krishna was attending in the south. I could live with Uncle Nandi, whom I greatly respected. His house was near the school.

"Rabi is coming! Rabi is coming!" It was Daadi's voice, announcing my arrival from a distance as always.

Small suitcase in one hand, sweating from the heat and humidity, I was trudging up from the bus depot to the house of Nandi Maharaj, my father's elder brother, in the southern part of the island. I enjoyed my periodic visits there. His wife, Daadi, was a very outgoing and excitable person and always welcomed me with happy shrieks as soon as she saw me in the distance. But this time I detected a note of alarm in her voice and soon discovered why. As I entered the house, my nostrils were immediately assailed by the distressing odor of goat curry. I had never suspected that they ate meat. What a shocking disillusionment!

"Oh! We didn't know you was coming here today!" Uncle Nandi seemed to be groping for words to hide his embarrassment.

"I wanted to give you all a surprise," I replied quietly, not knowing which way to direct my eyes, feeling his distress keenly. Oh, the shame! A Brahmin eating meat! And such a good and religious one!

My uncle tried to engage me in general conversation about Ma's health and news of other family members, but I answered coldly, making no attempt to hide my displeasure. At last the conversation died. Knowing what I was thinking, Uncle Nandi tried to justify himself. "You know why Christians does eat meat, Rabi?" he asked.

It seemed a strange question to me. What did it matter what excuses Christians gave for their crimes against my god the cow? I shook my head, feeling almost too nauseated to speak. How I wished I hadn't decided to give them the pleasure of a surprise visit.

"God let a big-big sheet down from the sky full up with all kinds of animals. . . ."

"Where you get that from?" I asked.

"Yeh, man, it in the Bible—the Christian book."

"You mean you does read *that?*"

"I don't read it myself, but I does hear about it."

"And what happen to the big-big sheet now?" I was becoming more angry and disillusioned. This was the same book Nana had thrown Ma down the stairs for reading. The book of Christians—the cow-eaters! And this was my father's brother!

"It had all kinds of animals in it—and you know what God tell Peter? He tell him to kill and eat as much as he like!" His face wore a look of triumph, as though he had demonstrated full justification for that horrible smell of violence and death in the house.

"Maybe," I said sharply, "but he not tell you!"

"But we do it in the name of Kali," Nandi added. "The temple priests does kill sixteen goat every morning at the famous Kali temple in Calcutta." My aunt was nodding her head from just inside the kitchen where she had taken refuge from my wrath.

"But the Brahmins don't *eat* them!" I reminded him sternly.

I wouldn't touch anything from their table all that day. The very odor of meat had polluted the entire house. People respected me for the principles I held, and for the fact that I stuck with them. At home I had my own plate and utensils, even my own pillow slip and sheets—and no one else dared to use them. I wouldn't eat bread or cake that had egg in it. Nandi knew this. Always in the past we had had so much to talk happily together about. Now we sat in an uncomfortable silence broken infrequently by a few awkward sentences. My aunt stayed out of sight, and so did my young cousins. At last my uncle suggested that we take a walk to the nearby harbor to look at a large Dutch oil tanker that had just come in the day before. I agreed, glad to have an excuse to get out of the house and away from its defiling odor.

The Dutch ship was a beauty, sleek and long and larger than any tanker I had ever seen. One could almost see it sinking deeper into the water as those huge pipes poured a steady stream of black gold from the barges that shuttled back and forth to where she lay just offshore. Near us on the wharf a cargo vessel was being loaded, long booms pointed out over the dock, winches screaming as heavy loads were hoisted into the air. Busy stevedores stripped to the waist were sweating profusely in the relentless sun. I had always loved visiting the harbor. The bustling activity sent a surge of excitement through me, and the strange names on the ships seemed a tantalizing call to visit faraway, exotic places. Nandi loved the harbor as much as I did. Without our noticing it, the tension between us gradually eased and we fell into a comfortable conversation about my plans to attend the nearby high school in the fall, which would make it possible for me to visit him more often. He seemed pleased and assured me that I was making the right decision, one that my father would have approved.

"But how come it ain't have nobody workin' on this boat?" I asked as we passed under the towering hulk of a freighter that appeared to be deserted.

"That really strange," replied my uncle thoughtfully, searching the ship with his eyes.

"Look at this!" I exclaimed, grabbing a heavy rope that hung down within a few feet of the dock from a jutting boom. I tested it with my weight. It seemed strong enough to hold several tons. "Look how I could do it! Just like Tarzan!" I yelled, taking a quick run and leaping into the air. Back and forth I went in a giant arc, clinging to the swinging rope, arching high above the dock, then swooping down past my uncle, who was laughing and enjoying the fun. Then it happened. At the top of the arc, as abruptly as if someone had cut it with a knife, the rope suddenly came loose from the boom high above me.

"Look out, Rabi!"

I heard my uncle's shout almost before I realized what was happening. Down I came, horrified to see that I was heading straight for the narrow opening between the ship and the dock. My flailing hands caught the edge of the wharf, where I hung precariously, half stunned. Grabbing me by one arm, Nandi hauled me to safety just as the ship lurched with the slow motion of the water and slammed against the dock.

"Boy you ain't play you lucky, nah!" he exclaimed. I could have been crushed. His lips were trembling and the color had drained from his face.

I was almost too weak to stand. We both stared dumbfounded at that serpentine coil of loose rope on the wharf, then up at the boom high over our heads. There seemed to be no explanation. The rope had been secure one instant and the next it was not, as though some unseen hand had suddenly untied it. An involuntary shiver ran up my spine as a flood of memories swept over me: of the time I had felt unseen hands shove me off a moving truck and I had been seriously injured; of that unforgettable morning when *something* unseen had held my foot down so that I couldn't pull it from the path of a heavy roller that had crushed it . . . and other similar "accidents." Now in the shadow of the strangely deserted ship I felt distinctly the menacing presence of Shiva that I knew so well. Had he untied that rope? I tried to reject the blasphemous thought, fearful of Shiva's wrath, but that sense of his presence lingered on. *Why?* I was not the meat-eater!

Sobered and solemn, we walked slowly back to the house in silence, both of us lost in thought. If this was my karma from a past life, then I felt it was terribly unjust. Why should I be punished for some past sin that I couldn't even remember?

SEVEN

Holy Cow!

"Exciting news, Rabi! I'll be teaching at Queen's Royal College in Port of Spain! Why don't you go there instead of down south?" Uncle Deonarine showed me the letter that had just come giving him the appointment.

"You really think I should?" It was frightening to imagine attending such a large and prestigious school.

"Of course! You could drive to school with me every day—keep me company. How about it?"

I was extremely fond of Uncle Deonarine. It would be great to drive with him every day, a chance to talk about so many things . . . so I agreed. What a thrill it was that first day to drive through Port of Spain's broad streets lined with busy shops and large red-roofed houses, past expansive parks with their green-turfed soccer fields and cricket clubs, to arrive at the impressive buildings of Queen's Royal College. Uncle Deonarine seemed no less pleased than I was and proudly introduced me straight off to several of the faculty as his "young Brahmin nephew."

Everyone gathered first of all in the large auditorium, where we were dealt a long and, to me, totally incomprehensible speech by the principal. I had heard few Englishmen speak and hadn't understood any of them clearly, but he was the worst of the lot. I hardly got a word.

"Ai, what he say?" I whispered to a student next to me when it was all over. I would need an interpreter to attend this school!

He looked at me strangely. "Are you *deaf?*" he asked loudly.

"No, I not *deaf*, but what he talkin' about?"

"Oh, just some regulations and stuff. I guess you're from down south . . . somewhere in the country?"

I nodded, beginning to wish I'd gone to that other high school with Krishna after all. Before the day was over I wished even more fervently that I'd never heard of Queen's Royal College. In the part of the island where I lived almost the entire population was East Indian, but in Port of Spain the overwhelming majority was black, and that created an immediate conflict within me. All my life I had nursed a deep hatred for black people, because they ate my god the cow. I counted them lower than the lowest caste. How could I bear to sit next to them in class, rub shoulders with them in the crowded halls of this high school, and play soccer with them? That first day my prejudice and pride received a number of sharp jolts. The only blacks I had ever known were the children of extremely poor laborers. These in the capital city were different. Many came from wealthy families and spoke better English than I did. Amused by my twangy country speech with its wrong pronunciation and bad grammar, other students snickered behind their books when my turn came to recite. With great effort I began to speak more properly to avoid ridicule.

In the weeks that followed, my daily contact with the many blacks, Orientals, pale English youths, and those of other races presented a serious challenge to my religious beliefs. The caste system is basic to Hinduism. Brahma himself had created the four castes from his own body—no government edict could change that statement in the Vedas—so there was no basis for even the existence of anyone else in the world. Yet the world *was* filled with other human beings who were completely outside of the caste system. How had *they* come into existence? Why was there no mention in the Hindu scriptures of a way of salvation for *them* through Yoga and reincarnation? Clearly they were without hope according to my religion. Yet they were in no way inferior to me. In fact,

I found it very difficult to compete with many of them in class. In my part of the island I was looked up to and deified. Indeed, I was sure that I *was* God. But these unenlightened boys at Queen's Royal College treated me as a mere equal, and sometimes not even as that. And the questions they asked—sometimes in jest, sometimes seriously—began to tear at the fabric of my faith.

"Is it true that Hindus believe *everything* is God?"

I nodded, glancing uneasily from the questioner to the boys of various races and religions who had gathered to bait me. It was getting to be a regular habit—and the other Hindu boys carefully avoided giving me any support, as though they were ashamed or afraid.

"You mean a fly is God, or an ant, or a *stink bug?*" A ripple of laughter spread through the small crowd standing around me.

"You laughin' because you don't understand," I said stoutly. "You see only the illusion but don't see the One Reality—Brahman."

"Are *you* God?" asked a Portuguese boy incredulously.

I dared not hesitate or hedge—that would only bring more ridicule. "Yes," I responded firmly, "and so are all Hindus. They just need to *realize* it."

"How're you going to 'realize' what isn't true?" he retorted with a derisive snort. "*You* didn't create the world!"

One English boy seemed to know too much about Hinduism. "I hear you're a vegetarian—don't believe in taking any life...."

"I believe in nonviolence. Like Gandhi. Everybody respects him. He was a great Hindu! It's wrong to take life."

"*Any* life?" I failed to notice the tone of his voice that should have warned me he was setting a trap.

I nodded emphatically. "*All* life is sacred. The Vedas say so." I looked appealingly to several Chinese boys in the group that I knew were Buddhists. They believed the same thing—why didn't they admit it? I knew that I was in trouble and wished they would help me on this point, although I was their enemy on many other religious points. Already in biology class I had learned that the seven characteristics of life were respiration, ingestion, elimination, irritability, growth, reproduction, and movement. And I knew all too well that even vegetables had every one of these characteristics. I was taking life when I plucked a banana or mango and ate it. I had found no way to deny that vegetarians take life, but I was determined to defend the difference between taking vegetable life and animal life.

My antagonist winked at his friends. "Don't you know that even vegetables have the seven characteristics of life?" he asked. "Vegetarians take life, too."

I opened my mouth to attempt to differentiate vegetable life from animal life, but someone else was already talking. "How about when he boils water for his tea?" said a voice behind me. "Think of all the millions of bacteria he kills then! Little *animals*—that's what they are. You know, they eventually evolve into cows and humans!"

Everyone had a good laugh at that. "Why, he's a regular murderer!" shouted a voice to my left. "No wonder he's so skinny!" added someone else. "Eating only vegetables! You've got to have meat, man!"

"You just don't understand!" I protested valiantly. My cheeks were burning and inside I felt bruised and confused.

"Don't try to make Hinduism logical or scientific," was Uncle Deonarine's advice that evening as we drove home. "It's a religion—something you choose to believe, not something you can prove."

"But truth is truth!" I insisted. "The Hindu scriptures are the Truth!"

"Much of what they say is pure mythology," said Deonarine in a patronizing tone. "Krishna never existed; neither did Rama. The *Bhagavad-Gita* and the *Ramayana* are just myths, beautiful stories."

I could see that it was useless to argue with Uncle

Deonarine. He had never been interested enough in his religion to practice Yoga, so he couldn't understand what I knew. He hadn't met some of the gods as I had. Perhaps it was his karma not to understand in this life. He would have many other lives in which to learn the truth when he was ready.

That evening as I grazed the cow under the coconut palms behind Gosine's hut, I watched her closely, as I had ever since that day when she had attacked me. It hardly seemed right not to trust such a great god, but one had to be practical. That was one of the things I was learning in high school—to be practical. Clearly one's religion must not be followed too literally in real life. I had ceased to worship the cow for practical reasons. It wasn't possible to guard against an attack and worship at the same time. But I would never stop believing in the cow as a great and holy god. In fact, I was sure it would be a great step upward toward union with Brahman to become a cow in my next life, if I failed to reach *moksha*.

"You are a god, aren't you?" I asked the cow very seriously.

She continued to tear great mouthfuls of the lush grass, chewing it slowly and with profound contentment. Hard indeed to believe that the cow could attack me so viciously, but the memory was still very clear.

"Of course you're a god! I know you are. Isn't that right?"

Raising her head, she stared at me with sleepy eyes and chewed her cud ever so slowly and peacefully. "Moo!" she declared solemnly. "Moo! Moo!"

EIGHT

Rich Man, Poor Man

"How did Nana get so rich?" I asked Uncle Deonarine one evening. Speculation on this subject continued to fascinate me and many others, but I had never heard Deonarine discuss it. We were standing on the front veranda enjoying the view of the brightly lighted houses across the town. Each Hindu family seemed to compete with its neighbors to see who could display the most *deyas* during the annual Divali festival.

"The pundits say it was the spirits that gave him the gold." Deonarine shrugged uneasily. "There really isn't any logical explanation," he added thoughtfully. "Of course Nana worked hard. Although a high-caste Kshatriya, he started out as a farm boy cutting para grass for ten cents a day. Somehow he bought a shack from a Chinese for fifty dollars and began making jewelry there. One night it burned down mysteriously . . . and after that he was a millionaire, although few outside of the family knew it."

As dusk turned to dark the sacred lights all around us seemed to grow brighter. What a beautiful sight! Divali was one of my favorite national holidays. To me it was inspiring to see every Hindu home glowing far more brightly than Christian homes at Christmas—and not with electric lights, but with live flames on the ghee-soaked wicks. Like bright candles, the *deyas* were flickering on windowsills, tables, porch railings, on steps from top to bottom—each in honor of Lakshmi, goddess of wealth and prosperity.

Uncle Deonarine waved a hand toward a particularly

well-lighted house. "Nana always did his own special *puja* to Lakshmi twice a day during Divali, alone in front of his big iron safe. There were other mystical rites in that room, too, but no one was ever allowed to observe them."

"What do you think? Was it Lakshmi that made him wealthy, or the spirits?" I asked. Our family pundit periodically went through each room of the house with a lighted *deya*, worshiping the house and the spirits in it—especially the spirit of Nana who had built it. He would solemnly wave the *deya* three times in a clockwise circle around Nana's large photograph in the living room. We revered the spirits as much as the gods, and sometimes there was almost a confusion of identity between them.

"Does it matter what you call it? Isn't there only one Force in the universe?"

I nodded solemnly. "There is only One Reality—Brahman. All else is illusion, maya."

We watched the lights in silence. One could almost feel the presence of Lakshmi and sense that she was pleased. But there was another question I had to ask, and finally I broke the silence.

"Some say that the same spirits that guard his fortune killed Nana before he could spend it. I don't understand that. What do you think?"

Uncle Deonarine didn't answer for several minutes. I waited impatiently. When at last he spoke, there was an uneasy note in his voice. "I don't know. Every time Divali comes, I think of my father's wealth, mysteriously acquired and mysteriously hidden beyond reach of any of us . . . and of his untimely death." He coughed nervously and turned to go back into the house. "I don't like to talk about such things," he added softly over his shoulder.

I remained there alone for a long time, watching the spectacular sight, marveling at how many *deyas* there were, and pondering the mystery of the many gods and spirits and the One Reality.

"The lights are burned to Lakshmi, and special *pujas* said to her. She is the goddess of wealth and prosperity." I was explaining the Divali festival to a Muslim boy as we sat eating our lunch together. He seemed interested, but as usual a small crowd of hecklers had gathered.

"If Lakshmi is the goddess of wealth and prosperity, how come most Hindus are so poor?" demanded a tall black boy. "It's a waste of time worshiping her!"

"You don't understand karma and reincarnation!" I retorted sharply. "A man can be poor in one life and wealthy in the next."

"How many reincarnations does it take? Look around! Most East Indians are cane-cutters, living in poor houses. . . ."

"My family isn't poor!"

"He means Indians in general," insisted a slight English youth. "Look at India—it's the most miserable country in the world!"

"Who says so?"

"My father. He lived there before I was born. There are more rats than people, and such poverty and disease!"

"Maybe when the British ruled it, but not since Independence!" A momentary murmur of approval swept the crowd pressing around us. Trinidad was struggling to get out from under British rule, and Independence was a word that lit a fire in every patriot's heart.

"People are starving in India, while the rats get fat and the sacred cows die of old age!" declared another boy, jumping into the fray. "That's what her gods and reincarnation have done for India. I'm an atheist. I wouldn't have such gods!"

"That's not true! My mother lives there, and she never writes about anything like that!"

I knew that my antagonists were right, but it would cost me too much to admit it. India's poverty was a subject my mother carefully avoided in her letters. She described the gardens, the brightly plumed birds and exotic animals, and the temples and festivals, and she told all about her guru—but never the condition of the people. Certain books I had read, however, left no question in my mind that the land of my religion was exceedingly poor. How could this be the result of thousands of years of Yoga, improving karma, and upward reincarnation toward oneness with Brahman? Why did the Indian movies I saw always avoid giving an honest picture of the country? And why did I persist in arguing with the boys at school on at least several points where it was so obvious that I was wrong? Was I afraid of the truth? I could never admit that—the implication involved too much!

"What make you think this world the onliest one?" asked Gosine when I delicately raised the question of why so many Hindus were poor and suffering. He kept the *deyas* burning to Lakshmi day and night in his mud hut during Divali, though he had told me that his karma was to be poor. "The Vedas say it have many worlds. Maybe it have only poor Hindus in this one. When they get better karma they go go to a better world."

"Yeh, but ain't they have rich Hindus here, too, like Nana and the pundits?"

Gosine nodded solemnly. "What I go say, *Bhai*, maybe it not work same for ev'rybody . . . but other worlds have only rich, maybe."

"Yeh, man, but in the *Gita* Krishna say that when karma worked out on other world you go come back here again."

"Some things not so easy to catch. . . ." Did Gosine's eyes betray a fleeting doubt? He recovered quickly. "For the Yogi rich and poor all same. Yogi, like your father, not go come back to this world—never. In the *Upanishads* it say that all ignorance go go away if they meditate on Brahman. They find *OM*. Only Yogis get this 'lightenment.'"

In referring to the *Vedanta* Gosine had expressed well my supreme goal. One of my most prized possessions was a book on yoga my mother had sent me from India. It contained advanced techniques that I was able to use by building upon the foundation of what I had learned at the temple. Lord

Krishna had taught Arjuna that there was nothing more important than the diligent practice of yoga. By this "divine raft" one could pass over ignorance and the most heinous sins to eternal Bliss. From the age of about ten, in addition to my daily meditation, I practiced yoga—the positions, breathing exercises, and meditation—on the veranda outside of my room from midnight to 1:30 A.M. when everyone else was asleep. I did either Brumadhya Drishti or Madhyama Drishti. This concentration, combined with the breathing exercises, projected me into realms of consciousness totally unrelated to the world around me.

Through yoga I experienced increasingly the presence of spirit beings who were guiding me and giving me psychic powers. The gods were *real!* All the arguments of the boys at school could not change that. Sometimes I would be too excited by these experiences to be able to sleep when finally I went to bed. If only I could get Deonarine and other Hindus to practice yoga and meditation—then they would know the truth about their religion. I must not enter nirvana alone. A guru is a teacher who leads others to eternal Bliss.

"Rabi! Rabi!"

I was alone in the prayer room sitting in front of the small figure of Lord Krishna, breathing deeply and rhythmically, trying to imitate Krishna's smile. Aunt Revati and I had quarreled bitterly again that morning, and yet I couldn't even remember how it had started. I was hoping, through meditation, to restore the sense of inner peace that seemed so elusive lately. But Ma and I were home alone, and there was no one else to answer when she called.

"What is it, Ma?" I yelled back.

"Somebody callin' downstairs. Go see who it be."

The family had gone to the beach for the annual Kartiknahan festival. Most Hindus in Trinidad were bathing in the rivers and bays in hope of spiritual cleansing. There was no bigger or busier or more profitable day for the pundits.

They'd be hurrying through one *puja* after another for the bathers, gathering in the fees and gifts and enjoying the food that everyone would share with them. It was a great day for improving one's karma by feeding Brahmins. I had begun to doubt the benefit of such rituals. Nothing could change one's karma—certainly bathing at Kartiknahan didn't. After drying off, many of these Hindus would go right back to eating meat and beating their wives. Such festivals had their place, but as Krishna had said, to the Yogi all else is meaningless. I had chosen a better way to spend my precious time.

"All right, Ma," I called. Reluctantly and carefully I wrapped Lord Krishna in his sacred cloth and put him away. Walking out on the veranda, I could hear someone knocking near the front steps. Leaning over the railing, I saw an elderly Indian beggar peering up at me.

"What you want?" I called down to him.

"*Roti*, Baba," he replied, stretching out his hand appealingly toward me. Was he honoring me, or using "Baba" as a poor Hindu's way of ingratiating himself with the rich? I pushed the question aside.

"Come up, na. I go see what it have." Begging was honorable.

Shaking his head, he pointed to his bare feet. "Me not able for climb up quite there!"

"Okay, man, come round to other gate." I pointed it out.

He looked like an Untouchable with very dark skin, someone I shouldn't even come near—it would be defiling to a Brahmin. But as I watched him move painfully along, leaning heavily on his walking stick, lurching and stumbling, I began to feel compassion for the old beggar. He was a human being, too. I felt good just admitting it. Hurrying down the back stairs, I unlocked the gate. Greeting him with a warm smile, I led him slowly to the open patio under the kitchen at the back of the house.

"Come sit here," I said, motioning to a chair beside a

table. He stared back at me coldly through large, round, unblinking eyes. With a gasp and a thud he dropped onto the chair. He ignored the water I gave him for washing his hands, apparently not interested in that. "I goin' to take out some food for you," I said pleasantly.

Exploring the kitchen, I found some leftovers from breakfast: the thin, pancakelike *roti* and some cooked spinach mixed with hot spices, called *bhaji*. Placing the food before him, I sat down to observe him with great interest. He was one of those traveling holy men, fairly common in our part of the island, who have renounced all possessions. Most had little to renounce. His long gray hair was uncombed and matted with dirt, and his beard had the remains of a variety of recently begged meals stuck among the unkempt hairs. The dhoti he wore, which apparently had once been white, was now gray and moldy, with numerous splotches of curry and sauces down the front. I had to shove my chair farther away —the odor he gave off was unbearable. Yet I felt a growing compassion for this repulsive fellow, and that gave me a sense of virtue. This would help my karma.

"You come from far today?" I asked, hoping to start him talking.

Chewing voraciously, the only response he gave me was a dark scowl. Tearing off pieces of *roti*, he dipped out large mouthfuls of *bhaji*, licking his fingers, obviously relishing every bit. I was sure I had brought too much—but he finished it all, wiping the dish clean. Taking a long drink, he leaned back in his chair, glared at me, and belched loudly. Wiping at his mouth with the front of his dhoti, he added fresh color to the older stains.

"Latrine!" he growled suddenly, and his large eyes darted desperately around as though he had to find it quickly. I jumped up to help him, and he grabbed at my shoulder, pulling himself out of the chair. Leaning half on me and half on his heavy stick, he shuffled along as I led him to the outhouse we kept in the back as an extra. When he had gotten clumsily inside, he ordered me to wait. Presently I heard him call, "Ai ya! Ai ya!" He sounded desperate.

"Yeh, what you want?" I answered uncertainly.

"Com' here!"

Hesitantly I opened the door. He couldn't get off the seat. Those cold eyes seemed to mock me. Leaning over, trying not to breathe, I grabbed him under the armpits and pulled with all my might while he grunted loudly but helped little. Finally he was on his feet again, swaying unsteadily, groping for his stick. He seemed unable to talk. Motioning and mumbling, he made me understand that he couldn't bend over far enough. Embarrassed, I reached down and pulled up his dhoti. I had long since passed my limit of breath-holding and was forced to take in deep gulps in spite of the horrible odor. He could not have had a bath in months. But he was a human being, and despite his cold stare and unfriendliness, I wanted to help him. Here was proof that I wasn't really selfish and a shirker like Aunt Revati accused me of being. It gave me a good feeling to be doing this, a feeling I hadn't had in a long time.

I led him toward a faucet, thinking he would want to wash, but he had no interest in that. He grunted indignantly, and those cold eyes lit up with the hatred that I should have noticed had been smoldering just beneath the surface all the time. He gave me a shove and lurched toward the gate, leaning on his stick, limping and waddling like some injured animal.

I reached the gate first and swung it open for him. He hobbled through, then turned and spat at my feet. Mute until now, suddenly he vomited out a torrent of the filthiest language imaginable in Hindi and English, expressing the hatred he felt that I possessed the things he had renounced. Did he really want what I had? Did he hate me because he thought I was rich and he was poor? I was confused . . . and stunned. Not even a "thank you" for what I'd done?

Closing and locking the gate mechanically, hardly knowing what I was doing, I hurried to wash myself thoroughly, then climbed the steps onto the veranda in a daze. Numbed and shaken, I didn't return to the prayer room to meditate. Krishna's blissful smile was forgotten. In my room, I sank miserably down onto the edge of the bed with head bowed. The beggar was right—poverty was more spiritual because riches are part of the illusion of ignorance. But then why was Lakshmi the goddess of wealth and prosperity if possessions were evil or merely maya? Why had she rewarded Nana with millions? And where was that gold now? Were the gods themselves, like all the temples erected in their honor, only part of a great illusion?

I was still sitting on my bed, head in my hands, reliving this nightmare, unable to cope with the devastating questions it forced upon me . . . when the family returned lightheartedly from their soul-cleansing excursion to the beach.

NINE

The Unknown God

When school closed at the end of my second year at Queen's Royal College, I went away as usual to spend several weeks vacationing at my Aunt Sumintra's ranch at Guara Cara in the highlands of the Central Range. I always enjoyed visiting her family—they treated me like a prince. There was nothing Aunt Sumintra wouldn't do for me. Her husband was serious and fairly industrious but also a heavy drinker, and he kept busy overseeing their large cacao plantation and a quarry they owned. Their son Sharma, a year older than I, had lived with us during school and was one of my closest friends.

I enjoyed being with my eight cousins, but most of all I loved the quiet and beauty of the mountains. It was good to get away from the din of jukeboxes, motorcycles, and automobile horns that so often disturbed my tranquillity in Port of Spain, And oh, how I loved nature! My deep sense of unity with the universe gave me a mystical feeling of identity with all living things: the many brilliant wild flowers, the endless varieties of chattering birds, the glistening leaves in the jungle after a thundershower. I was all of these and every creature that ran the forest trails. Each existed as one of my many bodies, and I was their higher awareness. The long walks I took each day through the paradise surrounding the ranch house left me with a sense of utter exhilaration. I was Brahman and this was my world, created by my thoughts.

As usual upon arriving there after that long, hot drive, I set right out upon a quiet walk, exulting in the beautiful scenery, absorbed in observing closely the unusual varieties of flora and fauna. Arriving at the edge of a jutting cliff deep in the jungle, I stood looking down upon a forest of salmon-hued immortelles spreading their royal canopy over the cacao trees in the valley below me. In the distance, on the other side of the plantation, tall feathery stands of bamboo swayed in the breeze; far beyond, the waving cane fields, barely visible in the haze, stretched like a green carpet to meet the blue of sea on the horizon. Behind me parrots, kiskadees, parakeets, corn birds, and other colorful species flitted back and forth in the treetops, chattering and scolding.

It seemed to me that the whole universe was singing the same song, throbbing with the same life, manifesting the same Essence. Every atom in everything, from the tiniest bacterium to the largest sun and farthest star, was an emanation from the same Source. All were part of the same great and only Reality. I was one with everything—we were all expressions of Brahman. Nature was my god and my friend. I became ecstatic with the joy of this universal brotherhood of all things and beings.

Chanting *"OM namah Shivaya"*—one must never forget one's duty to the Destroyer—I was turning a scorpionlike orchid in my fingers, admiring its pale, delicate texture and the incredible depth of its coloring that seemed to open up like the doorway into another world. Startled by an ominous rustling sound in the underbrush behind me, I turned quickly around. To my horror, I saw a large snake with thick body coming directly toward me, its beady eyes staring intently into mine. I felt hypnotized, paralyzed, wanting desperately to run but unable to move. Nor was there any way to escape, with the precipice at my back and the snake in front of me. Although the ugly reptile lacked the cobra's hood, I was struck by the resemblance it bore to that huge snake Shiva always wore around his neck—and I sensed the same presence that I so often felt in deep meditation, when I would find myself in a strange world sitting at Shiva's feet, his cobra companion hissing menacingly and darting out its tongue at me. The situation I now faced seemed like the destined fulfillment of these visions. This time I would not escape the Destroyer!

Close enough for me to touch it now, the snake raised its wide, wedge-shaped head above the grass and reared back to strike. In that moment of frozen terror, out of the past came my mother's voice, as though she were standing there, repeating words I had long forgotten: "Rabi, if ever you're in real danger and nothing else seems to work, there's another god you can pray to. His name is Jesus."

"Jesus! Help me!" I tried to yell, but the desperate cry was choked and hardly audible.

To my utter astonishment, the snake dropped its head to the ground, turned clumsily around, and wriggled off at a great rate into the underbrush. On trembling legs that threatened to buckle under me, I made a wide circle around the place where the snake had disappeared and stumbled through the thick jungle back to the path leading to the house. Breathless and still trembling, filled with wondering gratitude to this amazing god, Jesus, but afraid to mention his name, I told my startled cousin Sharma of my narrow escape.

My thoughts often returned to the puzzling question of who this Jesus really was. I remembered hearing about him in songs on the radio at Christmas, and knew that he must be one of the Christian gods. But I wondered why, when I had attended a primary school run by a Christian denomination, I had never heard anything about this Jesus that I could now recall. The only thing I remembered learning about Christianity was that the first people were named Adam and Eve, and someone named Cain killed his brother Abel.

I pondered that experience for days. Jesus was a powerful and amazing god. How quickly he had answered! But what was he the god of? Protection? Why had my mother—or the swami in the temple—not taught me more about him? I asked Gosine about Jesus, but he knew little if anything at all.

TEN

"And That Thou Art!"

During my third year in high school I experienced an increasingly deep inner conflict. My awareness of God as the Creator, separate and distinct from the universe he had made, an awareness that had been a part of me even as a small boy, contradicted the concept given to me by Hinduism that God was everything, that the Creator and the creation were one and the same. I felt torn between these two irreconcilable views. What I experienced in meditation agreed with the Vedic teaching about Brahman, but my experience of life at other times disagreed. In Yogic trance I felt a oneness with the whole universe; I was no different from a bug or cow or distant star. We all partook of the same Essence. Everything was Brahman, and Brahman was everything. "And that thou art!" said the Vedas, telling me that Brahman was my true Self, the god within that I worshiped sitting in front of a mirror.

It seemed difficult to face everyday life after hours in trance. The conflict and contrast between these two worlds was unresolvable. The higher states of consciousness I experienced in meditation were supposedly approaching reality as it really was. Yet the everyday world of joys and sorrows, pain and pleasure, birth and death, fears and frustrations; of bitter conflicts with my Aunt Revati and unanswerable questions posed by my classmates at Queen's Royal College; of holy men who stank and cursed, and of Brahmacharyas who fell in love

. . . was the world I had to deal with, and I dared not dismiss it as illusion unless I was prepared to call insanity true enlightenment. My religion made beautiful theory, but I was having serious difficulty applying it in everyday life.

Nor was it only a matter of my five senses versus my inner visions. It was a matter of reason also. The real conflict was between two opposing views of God: was God all that there was—or could he make a rock or a man without its being part of himself? If there was only One Reality, then Brahman was evil as well as good, death as well as life, hatred as well as love. That made *everything* meaningless, life an absurdity. It was not easy to maintain both one's sanity and the view that good and evil, love and hate, life and death were One Reality. Furthermore, if good and evil were the same, then all karma was the same and nothing mattered, so why be religious? It seemed unreasonable; but Gosine reminded me that Reason could not be trusted—it was part of the illusion.

If Reason also was maya—as the Vedas taught—then how could I trust any concept, including the idea that all was maya and only Brahman was real? How could I be sure that the Bliss I sought was not also an illusion, if none of my perceptions or reasonings were to be trusted? To accept what my religion taught I had to deny what Reason told me. But what about other religions? If all was One, then they were all the same. That seemed to deify confusion as the Ultimate Reality. I was confused.

My only hope was Yoga, which Krishna in the *Gita* promised would dispel all ignorance through the realization that I was not other than God himself. At times this inner vision had dazzled and excited me—I had felt so close to Self-realization that I could almost see myself as Brahman, the Lord of all. Almost, but not quite. I had told myself it was true and pretended that I was God; but always there had been that inner conflict, a voice warning of delusion. I had fought against this as the vestige of primordial ignorance, and at times had felt that I was on the verge of conquering this insidious illusion just as my father had. But never had I quite been able to bridge the chasm separating me and all of creation from the Creator.

I began to think of the Creator as the True God, in contrast to the many Hindu gods, some of whom I had met in my trances. I felt increasingly the stark difference between the terror *they* struck in my heart and the instinct I had that the True God was loving and kind. There was not one of the Hindu gods whom I now felt I could really trust. Not one that loved me. I felt a growing hunger to know the Creator, but I knew no mantras to recite to him, and I had the uneasy feeling that my pursuit of Self-realization was not bringing me nearer but taking me farther from him. It troubled me also that, in spite of my attempts to realize that I was Brahman, the feeling of peace I achieved in meditation never lasted very long in the everyday world—especially when I encountered Aunt Revati.

"Rabi Maharaj! Where have you been?" Aunt Revati cried in the scolding, querulous tone she so often used in addressing me lately. "I asked you to sweep down the stairs!" She was standing in the doorway of the kitchen as I walked past from the prayer room where I had just spent two hours in meditation. The blissful sense of inner peace I had enjoyed during that brief solitude was shattered by her voice.

"I'm going to do it—don't shout at me!"

"How else can I get your attention? You're always dreaming and in another world!"

"That's better than being in *your* world!" I muttered just loud enough for her to hear.

"Watch your mouth!"

"What about yours?" I retorted, this time under my breath.

Sweeping the steps outside, I thought to myself, Lord of the universe, Brahman thou art! It seems so real when I'm meditating, but with a broom in my hand . . . ?

"Hey, Rabi! We're goin' to the beach after lunch. Want

to come along?" My cousin Krishna, with whom I didn't get along very well either—he was so attached to his mother—was scrubbing the table and chairs on the patio, where I had fed the beggar several weeks before. Shouldering my broom, I walked idly toward him.

"Maybe," I responded without enthusiasm, "if Her Royal Highness don't expect me to sweep off the roof too!"

"Look here! You better watch your mouth, yes!" Aunt Revati had come down the steps to inspect my work and had walked up quietly behind me. "And too beside, you better go back and sweep over the steps—it still have black dust all over."

"I can't hold back the wind from blowing back the dust!" I replied angrily. A gentle breeze was stirring that carried the fine powder from the nearby sugar factory back onto the steps as fast as I swept it off. It wasn't my fault. Why couldn't she leave me alone?

"You lazy thing!" she scolded. "You lazy just like your father!"

Like my father? I let out an anguished cry that startled me. No one could talk about *him* that way! Years of smoldering hatred erupted like a volcano inside me. I became conscious of a set of barbell weights Nana had used to exercise with, resting in their familiar place only a step away. Blind with rage, scarcely conscious of what I was doing, I stooped over . . . and when I straightened up I had lifted the bar by one end as though it were a cricket bat. I swung the whole thing over my shoulder, taking aim for my aunt's head. As the weights arched up, from behind me Krishna made a desperate lunge and grabbed the other end. As though a spell had been broken, my superhuman strength vanished and the barbells fell with a sickening thud, smashing the thick concrete.

It seemed an eternity that I stood there staring into my aunt's ashen face. Her mouth had frozen half open, framing a wordless cry. I was shaking like a leaf in the wind. My eyes darted to the weights sunk into the concrete, then to Krishna, standing stunned behind me breathing heavily, fear showing in his eyes, then back to my aunt's stricken expression. The next thing I knew, I was running up the stairs, sobbing in loud gasps.

Reaching my room, I slammed the door and locked it behind me. Falling across the bed, I lay there for what seemed like hours, crying softly, unable to believe what had happened. My world had come to an abrupt end. I could never face my aunt again! Nor any other human being! Never!

I believed in nonviolence and had preached it like a Gandhi to my young Hindu friends. I was the strictest of vegetarians because I would not take any life and carefully avoided stepping on an ant or a bug. Then how could *I* have raised a hand against another human being, much less against my mother's sister? And how could *I* have lifted those weights like a club and swung them over my head as though they weighed nothing at all?

After midnight, when everyone was asleep and I should have been on the veranda seeking Bliss through Yoga, I crept quietly from my room, through the kitchen, and down the stairs to the patio. Groping my way in the darkness along the wall, I found the weights, still lying where I had dropped them. There was something I had to be sure of. Stooping over, I grabbed the bar with both hands—this time in the middle—arched my back and pulled with all my strength. I could not budge those weights—not an inch! With a convulsive sob, I turned back toward the stairs.

In my room again, I fell once more across the bed and wept quietly, face buried in my pillow. Where had the incredible strength come from to handle those heavy weights like a feather? Anger alone, even the wildest, could not account for that. Had I been possessed by one of the spirits I encountered in meditation? That whatever had lifted those weights was evil, I had no doubt. But I had been seeking union with

Brahman. Wasn't he evil as well as good, death as well as life, since he was All? Had I proven that at last? Was *this* my true Self—*"and that thou art!"*—this evil being of great power that had momentarily shed its veneer of religion? No! I could not believe that! I was horrified by what had happened. But how could I be sure that this evil force would not suddenly possess me again—perhaps with more tragic consequences the next time?

That question tortured me. Who were these gods and spirits and forces that I invited to come into me through *nyasa* and yoga and meditation? Were they evil or good or both— or was everything maya and I insane to try to make sense out of it? For several days I remained in my room, refusing all efforts to coax me out for a meal or even for a drink. And when at last I did try to face the world again—that world of illusion that was supposed to be unreal but which gave me so much trouble—I could scarcely look it in the eye. I said little to anyone. Aunt Revati and I avoided one another. There were no more orders directed at me about chores around the house. My morning visits to Ma were brief and strained.

Eventually, however, as I had hoped, time seemed to veil even this horrible episode in my life with a dulling sense of distance. Aunt Revati and I still avoided one another as much as possible, but when the occasion arose I was able to look at her, to say whatever necessity demanded in a fairly pleasant tone, and she showed no continuing resentment, at least not outwardly. The most troubling effect that lingered on was a new difficulty in convincing myself that I was Brahman . . . and a deep, unresolvable uncertainty as to who or what Brahman and the many gods I worshiped really represented or were. And who was *I*?

My goal of Self-realization had suffered a serious setback.

ELEVEN

Guru Puja

"There are too many hypocrites! All this talk of Self-realization . . . and they just become more selfish!"

I hesitated outside the door to Ma's room. Uncle Deonarine's angry words, so unlike him, shocked me. He had never talked like that in my presence. Was he referring to *me?*

"Plenty good pundits. What about Baba?" responded Ma quietly.

"How do I know he's not a hypocrite, too? It's a business with *all* of them—they do nothing without pay. *Nothing!*" The anger in my uncle's voice cut me like a knife. I had never guessed that he held such deep resentments. Why had he asked me to bless his car—and insisted upon paying me?

"You are paid for teaching at the school. Why should the pundits work for nothing?"

"But some pundits are so *rich!* They get so much money —and mainly from the poor. How many hundreds of good-luck *pujas* are said for a sweepstakes, but how many come out winners? The pundits know everyone can't win, but still they take everyone's money! If it weren't being done in the name of religion, those hypocrites would be put in jail for fraud!"

"But the poor pundits, what they go do?" asked Ma. "People does ask them to do *puja* and they does do it."

"Of course! That's their business. And when most people don't win—the odds take care of that—the pundits say it's their karma, something they did wrong in their last *janma*. If you rely on Baba's *pujas*, your chance of getting to heaven is the same as winning the next sweepstakes!"

"Shh. You're talking too loud. Someone will hear."

"Perhaps the whole world should hear!" he replied in a quieter voice.

Stunned by my uncle's attack upon the very heart of my religion, I quietly tiptoed away. I had thought that Uncle Deonarine was becoming favorable toward Hinduism again. Certainly he had never given me a hint that he felt like this. He was trying to be too logical, the very thing he had cautioned me against. One could not make a science out of religion. I must persuade him to begin the practice of daily meditation. It was the only way out. Lord Krishna was right, of course. If one really practiced yoga, nothing else mattered.

On the way to school that morning, however, Uncle Deonarine was full of Utopian talk about the miraculous transformation a progressive educational system would make in Trinidad. This was the enlightenment that he believed in. It was impossible for me to turn the conversation to Yoga. More clearly than ever I saw that he and I were poles apart. He was eager to tackle problems in a world I saw as maya—problems that the Vedas said could only be solved by denying they existed and treating them as pure illusion. He enthusiastically advocated education of the masses in Western science and technology as the only way Trinidad could become prosperous once Independence was achieved. How could I discuss with such a man the inner enlightenment a guru must achieve within himself and pass on to his followers? The tension between the world I experienced in deep meditation and the world I had to confront at all other times seemed almost to reach the breaking point that morning. There was no way I could share my inner conflict with Uncle Deonarine—at least not then—so I listened quietly and pondered what he said.

During school hours, mixing with boys of many races

and religions, I could almost forget for a short while my deep inner conflict. Outwardly I was happy at school, where I now had many friends. The boys no longer baited me with difficult religious questions. Like every other Trinidadian, I loved cricket and soccer and joined enthusiastically in the daily games even though such competition brought me into bodily contact with non-Hindus, a class of people nonexistent as far as the Vedas were concerned and thus even lower than the Untouchables. There were the usual bruises and cuts suffered at the hands of my schoolmates, all in good-natured sport. Then one afternoon the unexpected happened. In the midst of a routine soccer game, running across the field in hot pursuit of the ball, I found myself suddenly on the turf, writhing in agony, a hot, searing pain shooting through my lower abdomen. Classmates and the teacher on duty gathered around quickly.

"Nobody kicked him, how come he fell down? What's the matter?" someone asked. I could only answer with groans.

"Get him into the shade," said the teacher. Swimming in a sea of pain, I felt hands lifting me, then everything went black.

The ride in Uncle Deonarine's car was a blur of dreamlike motion and agony. In the doctor's office I lost track of time and voices. The last thing I remembered was hearing the doctor say something about "another few minutes and the appendix would have burst." I awakened hours later under clean white sheets in a hospital room minus part of my intestines, that pain in my side still there but throbbing now to a slower beat.

"You were lucky, Rabi!" Uncle Deonarine exclaimed with evident relief when he visited me the next day. "The doctor said it was a close shave."

On the third day and feeling much better, I was allowed to get up and go to the toilet on my own. Opening the bathroom door to return to bed, I felt an excruciating jolt of pain hit my right side. The room began spinning crazily and growing dark. Fighting to keep from losing consciousness, I grabbed wildly for the door handle but didn't find it. The blurred memory of a small jungle clearing on the edge of a cliff and something my mother had told me years before came back again.

"Jesus, help me!" I cried.

I felt a hand grip my arm and hold me up, though I knew there was no one in the bathroom. The darkness lifted. The room stood still once more. My eyes focused. Every twinge of pain had vanished, and in its place a remarkable feeling of well-being and strength surged through me.

Back in bed, I lay motionless for a long time, trying to understand what had happened. It was hard to believe, yet it was true. A strange calm had settled in the room. I fell into a deep sleep. When I awakened I noticed that someone had left a small Christian tract on my bedside table, the first one I had ever seen. Written by someone called Oswald J. Smith that of course I had never heard of, it was about a young man who had become a follower of Christ. It moved me deeply, but my mind was too crowded with the world of Hinduism to really understand. Jesus was soon forgotten again. I already had too many gods to worship all of them properly, so adding one more to the list would only have increased my burdens. Indeed, I often struggled with the problem of which god I should worship the most. I feared them all, but I divided most of my attention between Shiva and Krishna.

Each evening after arriving home from school, I would retire into the prayer room—my holy place. At exactly 6:00 P.M., with deep feeling, almost as though I were creating life, I would solemnly light the sacred *deya* flame on the second step in the very center of the altar. Before sitting down on the floor in lotus position for meditation and contemplation of the gods, I would perform my *arti*. Ringing a small bell with my left hand, on my right I balanced the large brass plate with the lighted *deya* in the center surrounded by fresh flowers, moving it in a clockwise circular motion three times around each deity, while repeating the appropriate mantra. One evening, something horrible happened. While doing the *arti* in front of Shiva, I accidentally bumped Krishna with my elbow, knocking the great god from the altar onto the floor!

Horrified, I quickly picked up the small brass figure. Caressing it gently, I discovered to my dismay that the fall had bent Krishna's flute and an arm. What consternation swept over me! I held Krishna tightly over my heart, feeling so remorseful, wanting to say I was sorry, yet knowing that no apology would be accepted. There could be no forgiveness. The unchangeable law of karmà forbade it. The payment that would be demanded of me in my next life—or perhaps even in the present one—for such a heinous crime was something I dared not imagine. No doubt the penalty would be severe. Yet if that little brass figure had such great power within it, why did it fall so easily? In view of the obvious helplessness of these little idols, my abject fear of them began to seem absurd.

In spite of unanswerable questions and the deepening conflict I felt, every waking moment that I wasn't at school or doing homework—and I did too little of that—I spent in zealous pursuit of my religious duties. I could only hope that my continued faithfulness would be recognized and rewarded, although Self-realization had now become for me more of a dream than a hope. I meditated as much as ever and still experienced heavenly music, psychedelic colors, astral travel, and spirit visitations in my trances. But that sense of being Brahman, Lord of the universe, the great Mind embodied in many forms, which had excited me for years, now eluded me. *Moksha* seemed an impossible goal for the present life. I was fearful that it would take many more reincarnations —I didn't know how many. Why did the future have to be so uncertain?

My father's achievement seemed more awesome than ever. Truly he must have been an avatar. Obviously I was not.

I was determined to be a great guru, and in the eyes of many I already was. But I would not reach nirvana in this life. My alternate goal—to be reincarnated as a cow, holiest of creatures—had been shattered too. Nothing was certain. But I would never admit my doubts to anyone. Outwardly I was as sure of my religion as ever, and the honor I received from Hindus was growing.

At the end of my third year in high school, Ma and Aunt Revati invited a large group of neighbors and relatives to join us in a special *puja* in our home. Those arriving approached to make their respectful bows and to reminisce a bit upon my father's greatness. Their comments, overheard here and there as the room filled, bore out the admiration I read in their appraising eyes. I was a Yogi who would bring fame to our town, a guru who would one day have many, many followers. My inner conflicts were forgotten in the sheer pleasure of being worshiped. Although I was not quite fifteen, I knew that already I had attained a status among Hindus that was the envy of some pundits. It gave me a good, honest feeling to know that I was not among the hypocrites my Uncle Deonarine despised.

Our Baba, Pundit Jankhi Prasad Sharma Maharaj, my spiritual adviser and greatest inspiration, the acknowledged Hindu leader for all of Trinidad, performed the elaborate ceremony. Proudly I assisted. It was a great occasion for me.

Fingering a large, fragrant garland of flowers around my neck, I stood near the altar greeting the guests after the ceremony. A neighbor laid several pieces of money one after another at my feet, and bowed to receive my blessing—the Shakti pat that every worshiper craved because of its supernatural effect. I knew her to be a poor widow who earned pitifully little for her long hours of hard labor. The offerings I received at one ceremony would far exceed her wages for a month. The gods had decreed this system of giving to Brahmins, and the Vedas declared it to be of great benefit to the giver, so why should I feel guilty? Uncle Deonarine's words rose vividly before me in all their venom: *"It's a business with all of them, they do nothing without pay . . . mainly from the poor!"* I glanced at her small offering of coins uncomfortably.

Of course I had much to give her in exchange. Reaching out to touch her forehead in bestowal of my blessing, I was startled by a voice of unmistakable omnipotent authority: "You are not God, Rabi!" My arm froze in midair. *"You . . . are . . . not . . . God!"* The words smote me like the slash of a cutlass felling the tall green cane.

Instinctively I knew that the true God, the Creator of all, had spoken these words, and I began to tremble. It was a fraud, a blatant deception to pretend to bless this bowing woman. I pulled back my hand, acutely aware that many eyes were watching and wondering. I felt that I must fall at the holy feet of the true God and ask his forgiveness—but how could I explain *that* to all these people! Abruptly I turned and pushed my way through the crowd, leaving that poor woman staring after me in bewilderment. Inside my room, I locked the door, tore the garland of flowers from around my neck with trembling fingers, flung it to the floor, and fell across my bed, sobbing.

Ma had seen me leave and had looked at me with compassion, a kindness I didn't deserve. I had not spoken to her for nearly a month. In her sweet way she had reproved me ever so gently for an angry argument I had provoked with my aunt. It had been clearly my fault, a shameful exhibition of self-righteous pride before the whole family. I had rejected Ma's pleas to apologize. Instead, I had stormed from her room shouting that I would never speak to her again. She had sent my cousins one by one to my room with fruits and other gifts, pleading for a reconciliation, but I had spurned every offer. Now I choked on that bitter memory as I lay broken under the reproof of the true God, conscience-stricken that I had dared to accept the worship which only he deserved. My whole world of pride was crumbling.

I wanted to tell this God that I was sorry—sorry for the way I had treated my aunt and Nanee and so many other people, and most of all sorry for the way I had robbed him by taking to myself the worship of men that only he deserved. But I didn't know how to address him, and surely there could be no forgiveness anyway. The law of karma would repay me what was due. A crime such as I had committed would make a disaster of my next reincarnation. It might be thousands of rebirths before I reached the Brahmin caste again— even millions. Who could foretell the painful path I must follow to climb back so far?

As horrible as my future seemed, facing the present was even more painful. I could never again accept the worship of another human being, yet it was expected of me. How could I avoid it? And how could I ever find the courage to admit to those who had put me on a pedestal that I was a thief who had stolen the glory that belonged only to One who was above us all? There was no way that I could ever leave my room to face the Hindu community again. They would not believe me if I tried to tell them that no man is God or worthy to be worshiped. And how could I tell them what I knew to be the miserable truth about myself? The shame would be too great! But I could not continue to live a lie, either. There seemed only one escape—to commit suicide. Again and again I came back to the horrible alternative that now seemed the only way out. How *this* would affect my next life I could only guess, but I feared the present even more.

Day after agonizing day I remained in my room without eating or drinking—pacing the floor, wringing my hands, falling exhausted on the bed for snatches of fitful sleep, only to pace the floor once again or to sit on the edge of my bed, head in hands. At times I wept, wishing I had never been born, beginning to pity myself. So much had gone wrong for me. I had missed the love and tender care of parents. My father had never spoken to me and had died when I was young. I hadn't seen my mother in eight years. I had lost my grandparents—all except Nanee. And I had once felt proud that my karma was so good! But why should it be so bad? It was unfair to punish me for past lives when I could not remember one single incident from any of them, although I had tried and even at times pretended that I could.

During those long, lonely hours I went back over the life that I could remember and wondered at my blindness. How could a cow or a snake—or even *I*—be God? How could the creation create itself? How could everything be of the same Divine Essence? That denied the essential difference between a person and a thing, a difference I knew was there, no matter what Lord Krishna and the Vedas said. If I was of the same *essence* as a sugarcane, then *essentially* there was no difference between me and sugarcane—which was absurd.

This unity of all things that I had experienced in meditation now appeared preposterous! Pride alone had blinded me. I had wanted so much to be Lord of the universe that I had been willing to believe an obvious lie. What could be more wicked than that? It was hypocrisy of the worst kind!

Day after day, I, who had once thought myself on the verge of Self-realization, now groveled in abject self-condemnation. I thought of all the cigarettes I had stolen, the lies I had told, the proud and selfish life I had lived, the hatred in my heart toward my aunt and others. There had been times when I had even wished her dead, yet at the same time I had preached nonviolence. There was no way my good deeds could ever outweigh the bad on any honest scale. I trembled at the thought of reincarnation, certain that my karma would drop me to the bottom of the ladder. How I wished that I could somehow find the true God so that I could tell him how sorry I was—yet what was the point of it since karma could not be changed? Perhaps he would be merciful.

I now feared the astral travel and the spirit visitations I had once exulted in, but I knew no other way to search for God than through yoga. My religion, my training, my experience in meditation—all had taught me that only by looking within myself could I find Truth, so I tried it again. The search within, however, proved futile. Instead of finding God, I only stirred up a nest of evil that made me even more aware of my own heart's corruption. My misery only became greater, my sense of guilt and shame a burden impossible to bear.

If I could not find this God soon, then I must commit suicide, no matter how severe the consequences of that cowardly act upon my future. I could not bear to live any longer without him.

I was afraid, however, to take my own life. My next life could well be worse than the present one. The future was all uncertainty and darkness. I had to somehow salvage my sanity in the present.

On the fifth day I bathed, ate some breakfast, and returned to my room without speaking to anyone. But I left the door open for the first time. It was a gesture that I hoped the family would understand, a step toward reconciliation, tentative and weak, but the best a very proud and self-righteous person could make without help.

TWELVE

Karma and Grace

"Rabi, there is someone here to see you." Shanti was standing just inside my room. I had not heard her approach.

"Who is it?"

"A friend of mine from school. She wants to talk with you."

An attractive young woman of about eighteen was seated in the dining room waiting for me. I hesitated in the doorway, looking at her questioningly. Seeing me, she jumped to her feet and her face lit up with a smile that seemed to come from deep within. She doesn't understand much of life, I thought, or she wouldn't be so happy.

"Hello, Rabi, I'm Molli," she said warmly. "I've heard a lot about you and I've been wanting to talk to you."

"Oh? What about?" I asked. "Sit down," I added impatiently and seated myself across the table from her. I had no time for her. What could she want with me? Why didn't Shanti visit with her? She had apparently gone to the kitchen.

Molli laughed good-naturedly at my puzzled expression. "I've heard how religious you are, and I wanted to meet you."

She asked me about myself and whether I found my religion fulfilling. Trying to hide my emptiness behind many words about my great knowledge of Hinduism, I lied to her and told her that I was very happy and that my religion was the Truth. She listened patiently to my pompous and sometimes arrogant pronouncements. Without contradicting or arguing, she exposed my emptiness gently with politely phrased questions.

At last she asked, "Do you have any special goal in religion?"

"Yes," I replied, "I want to get close to God."

"Do you know him?"

"Yes!" I lied, trying to hide my uncertainty. I knew he existed but I had no image of him, knew no mantras to recite to him, and had not found him through yoga. "Are you also a religious Hindu?" I asked, trying to turn the attention away from my own emptiness. She must worship the gods a great deal to have such peace.

"No. I used to be, but now I'm a Christian."

"You're *what?*" I was appalled.

"A Christian. I discovered that one can know God and draw very close to him through Jesus Christ."

"I believe that I can draw close to God through my own religion!" I exclaimed vehemently, knowing in my heart that it was a lie. In fact, I had discovered that each step closer to the Hindu gods was a step farther from the true God I sought. But I would never admit that—especially to a Christian! It was not the name Jesus Christ that upset me but the very word "Christian" and the thought that she had become one. They ate my god the cow. And most people I had known who called themselves Christians lived in such a way that I wanted nothing to do with their religion.

I rose from my chair to tell her to leave. There was no point in continuing the conversation. But she said something, very quietly, that made me sit down again. "The Bible teaches that God is a God of love. I would like to share with you how I came to know him."

I was stunned. Never in all my years as a Hindu had I heard of a God of love! I listened in amazement as she continued.

"Because he loves us, he wants to draw us close to himself." That staggered me again. As a Hindu I was wanting to get close to God, but she was telling me that God in love was trying to draw me close to him!

"And the Bible also teaches that sin is a hindrance not only to getting close to God," Molli continued, "but to knowing him at all. So he sent Christ to die for our sins. And if we receive his forgiveness we can know him—"

"Wait a minute!" I interrupted. Was she trying to convert *me*? I felt that I had to make some rebuttal. "I believe in karma. Whatever you sow you reap, and no one can change that. I don't believe in forgiveness at all. It's impossible! What's done is done!"

"But God can do anything," said Molli confidently. "He has a way to forgive us. Jesus said, 'I am the way, the truth, and the life: no man cometh unto the Father, but by me.' Jesus is the way. Because he died for our sins, God can forgive us!"

That was dogmatism I refused to accept. I had always insisted that Hinduism was the only way, but now I argued that the *Gita* said all roads lead to the same place and that whatever a man does, even without any religion, karma and reincarnation will eventually bring him to Krishna. But was it any less dogmatic to say that Krishna was the only destination than to say that Christ was the only way? And was Krishna what I really sought? No. In my heart I knew that he was not the true God whom I wanted to know. But I was too proud to admit that and continued to argue in favor of the many contradictory concepts of Hinduism, trying to save face. In spite of her patience—or perhaps because of it—I lost my temper and gestured angrily, raising my voice, determined not to be defeated by this girl. But she was so calm, and seemed so confident of her relationship to God, that at last I had to find out her secret.

"What makes you so happy?" I asked her suddenly. "You must have been doing a lot of meditation!"

"I used to," Molli replied, "but not any more. Since I received Jesus into my life he's changed me completely. He has given me a peace and joy that I never knew before." Then she looked me straight in the eye and said, "Rabi, you don't seem very happy. Are you?"

I glanced quickly around. Dishes were rattling in the kitchen. I lowered my voice. "I'm not happy. I wish I had your joy." Was I saying this? I had thought I could never share this secret even with Ma—and here I was sharing it with a stranger. And how could she help me? It was more than joy that I wanted. I had to know God!

"Joy isn't something you can produce," said Molli. "If there isn't a genuine reason for it, then it isn't real and won't last. My joy is because my sins are forgiven, and that has changed my whole life. Peace and joy come from Christ, through really knowing him."

"Don't keep talking about Jesus!" I interrupted impatiently. "He's just one of the gods—there's millions of them—and a *Christian* god at that. I want to know the *true* God, the Creator of the universe!"

"But that's who Jesus is. That's why he could die for your sins—only God could pay that debt." She was so calm, and spoke with such quiet confidence. My own attitude was such a contrast. I could never feel the confident trust toward the Hindu gods that she had for this god Jesus. She spoke of him as though he were a personal friend sitting right there beside her.

We talked for nearly half a day, not realizing how the time passed. I argued and lost my temper frequently and at times raised my voice at her. I had been losing my cool more and more these past months. Through it all she remained calm, unruffled, speaking with that quiet assurance. I continued to parade before her the Hindu gods and marshaled the philosophies of the ancient seers; but there was no way I could argue with what she *was*. I wanted her peace and joy, but I was not going to give up any part of my religion! She hadn't said anything about that, but I could see that if I believed that Jesus was God and that he had died for me and could forgive my sins, then everything I had lived for as a Hindu became meaningless.

"I really should go," she said at last and stood to leave.

I jumped to my feet, determined to make it clear that she had not changed my mind. Her visit was an outrage. I, a Brahmin, had condescended to speak with a reprobate who had left her religion—and she had had the audacity to attempt to persuade *me*, a Yogi, to become a Christian!

"Oh, I *hate* Christians!" I declared loudly and angrily so those in the kitchen could hear. "I'll *never* become a Christian —not even on my deathbed! I was born a Hindu, and I'll die a Hindu!"

She looked at me with compassion. "Before you go to bed tonight, Rabi, please go on your knees and ask God to show you the Truth—and I'll be praying for you!" With a wave of her hand she was gone.

Through the open doorway I could see the sun sinking lower over the Gulf. It would soon drop behind Punta Peñas on the northern tip of Venezuela and darkness would descend swiftly. Looking down at my hands, I saw that they were clenched, fingernails biting into my palms.

Alone in my room once again, I paced the floor, feeling that two armies were doing battle within. Never had I experienced such deep conflict. I seemed to face a choice between life and death and was being torn apart by forces that were pulling me in both directions. Throughout my conversation with Molli the conviction had gripped me that this true God must be holy and pure. How could he have anything to do with me? How well I had come to know the darkness of my heart. At last I confessed to myself, reluctantly, that all of my holy baths and *pujas* and yoga could never change that.

Wouldn't it be wonderful, I thought, if what Molli had said about Jesus dying for my sins was true, so that I could be forgiven and be cleansed in order to have fellowship with this Holy God! I wanted to believe it—but Jesus was a Christian god, and I would *never* become a Christian. If I did, I could not face my family again. Nor could I face life if I remained the way I was. I had struggled for Self-realization, looking within, trying to realize that I was God. I had only realized that I was hopelessly lost.

"They talk a lot about Self-realization . . . but only become more selfish!" Uncle Deonarine's words came back to haunt me. He had spoken the horrible truth! No wonder Ajah had been driven to destroy himself with rum because of his disillusionment with Hinduism. I had always refused to believe that, but at last I understood. Only my fear of what lay beyond death kept me from suicide.

Molli had insisted that God loved me and that she experienced his love. I envied her for that—but hated her for being a Christian. Pride demanded that I reject everything she had said, but I was too desperate to save face any longer. I fell to my knees beside the bed, conscious that I was giving in to Molli's request. Was she praying for me at that very moment?

"God, the true God and Creator, please show me the *Truth!* Please, God!" It was not easy to say, but this was my last hope.

Something snapped inside of me, like a tall bamboo broken by a gale. For the first time in my life, I felt I had really prayed and gotten through—not to some impersonal Force, but to the true God who loves and cares.

Too tired to think any longer, I crawled into bed and fell almost instantly asleep. My last conscious thought was a deep conviction that God had heard and would answer my prayer.

THIRTEEN

Enlightenment!

"Hey, Rabi!" said Krishna, coming into the kitchen where I had been conversing with one of my younger aunts while she cooked supper. His manner and the look on his face were so different from what I was used to seeing. He seemed pleased to have found me. "Did you know that you've got to be born again to get into heaven?" he asked.

I started to say, Of course. I'm going to be born again into a cow. That's my heaven! But Krishna's earnest expression made me swallow my sarcasm. "What makes you say that?" I asked skeptically. I noticed that he had a small black book in his hand and was turning the pages as though he were looking for something.

"It says so in the Bible. Let me show you." He continued turning the pages slowly, like one exploring unfamiliar territory. ". . . Mark . . . Luke . . . John. Here it is, in chapter three. Listen to *this!* 'Jesus answered and said unto him, Verily, verily, I say unto thee, Except a man be born again, he cannot see the kingdom of God.' What do you think of *that?*"

I didn't know what to think. Could this be the same Jesus my mother had told me about long years ago, the same one Molli claimed was the true God who had died for my sins? He must be!

"Let me see that!" I said, feeling excited now.

Krishna held the little book out to me so I could read it

myself—and as I read I understood at last what I'd been struggling to grasp for three weeks since Molli had talked to me. My world had been falling apart, but now everything seemed to fall into place. To be "born again"! Yes, that was what I needed. I knew exactly what Jesus meant. He was talking not about reincarnation but about a spiritual birth that would make Nicodemus into a new person on the inside instead of just giving him a new body.

Now I was really excited. Why had I never understood this before? What good would a thousand physical births do? Reincarnation could give me a new body, but that wasn't what I needed. I could not imagine a physical birth better than my present one. I had been born into the highest caste, into a wealthy family, the son of a Yogi, given all the advantages of education and religious training, and yet I had failed. It was folly to think that I would improve by coming back into this world in different bodies again and again!

Each New Year's Eve, like everyone else, I would make my New Year's resolutions. Always at the top of the list was the resolve to stop smoking. My cough had gotten worse, yet I couldn't quit. I would begin each January with a fresh determination to make the coming year an improvement over the last. But by January 2, I was always back to the old habits again. And it wouldn't be many more days before my ungovernable temper had exploded anew—often just after I had spent an hour or two seeking peace in meditation. There was something wrong with *me* that changing the body I lived in would never solve.

Wonderful as it would be if God really could forgive me, I had begun to long for more than forgiveness. Since asking God to show me the Truth, I had gradually seen myself in a new light. The world had always revolved around *me*. I had expected everyone to adjust their way of life to *my* desires and to treat *me* like a god. I was a spoiled tyrant, but I certainly wasn't God! Nor would I ever be. It had been a relief to admit it. I no longer wanted to be God. But I didn't want to remain the way I now saw myself. I wanted to become a new person. If Christ couldn't change me completely, then I didn't care to have his forgiveness.

In the past I had sought mystical experiences as an escape from the daily life which Hindu philosophy called maya—an illusion. Now I wanted the power to face life, to live the life God had planned for me. I wanted to experience a deep change in what I *was*, not merely the superficial peace I *felt* during meditation but which left me the moment I lost my temper. I needed to be born again—spiritually, not physically.

Conversation at the table that evening centered around a letter that had just arrived from Uncle Lari in Montreal, Canada, where he was studying philosophy on a scholarship at McGill University. He had gotten the highest score in the entire island on the Cambridge higher school certificate exams. We were all proud of him and eager to learn of his progress. From Lari the conversation turned to Krishna's future, and Uncle Deonarine urged him to follow in Lari's footsteps. Perhaps he could get a scholarship to a university in London. I was too busy with my own thoughts to contribute much to the family table talk. There was something I had to tell them, and I was trying to find the right words. In less than a week it would be my fifteenth birthday. What an appropriate day to be born again!

Everyone rose to leave the table, and I was still struggling for words. Deonarine and Krishna were about to carry Ma into the sitting room. I had to tell them *now*, but I was afraid. Well, they didn't need to know everything—not yet.

"Ma!"

"Yes, Rabi?" Her expression was so expectant. Was I going to accept her pleas for reconciliation? Was I softening? She didn't know how badly I wanted to.

"I don't want to have any celebration on my birthday."

"Rabi!" protested Shanti. "You don't mean that!"

"Why, Rabi?" asked Ma gently. "You know how we all look forward to your birthday the whole year." Her eyes conveyed so much love and sympathy. No doubt she thought that my request stemmed from the problem between us.

"It's nothing like you think," I said. "I just want it to be *different* this year." That was the end of the matter. My word was law on all religious and ceremonial matters.

How slowly those few days passed, but at last my birthday arrived. I didn't go near the prayer room, where I was expected to spend most of the day. The family must have wondered at that, but I was afraid to explain why. I was going to invite Jesus into my life and be born again. Such a wonderful thing to do on my birthday!

In spite of my resolve, however, I lacked the courage to fulfill it. What would my mother think if I became a Christian? And what about the pundits who had encouraged and trained me, and the Hindus who had worshiped me and given me gifts and trusted me to lead them to a higher reincarnation? How could I betray all of them? What would Gosine say? And the many neighbors who looked to me as an example for their children to follow?

The moment I asked Christ to be my Lord and Savior I would lose everything: my Brahmin caste, my status as a young Yogi, the blessing of the Hindu gods, the goodwill of my family. I would automatically be an outcaste from the Hindu community, lower than the lowest. *And* what if Jesus couldn't really forgive my sins and change my life after all? Suppose I couldn't really know God through him? How could I risk so much when I wasn't sure?

And so my birthday came and went, the day on which I had planned to be born again—and still I was afraid to open my heart to Jesus. When I fell asleep that night I was more miserable than I had ever been.

FOURTEEN

Death of a Guru

"*Namahste, namahste,* Yogi Rabindra Maharaj!"

I looked up from the book I was reading—Bertrand Russell's *Why I Am Not a Christian*—to see the tall, lean figure of Bhaju Radhaj Govinda bow toward me, then start up the back steps. I was thankful that the part of the veranda I was sitting on was not accessible to him except through the house. Once inside he would doubtless become caught up in conversation with Ma and Aunt Revati and never reach me. An old friend of the family from nearby Kali Bay, Govinda was a frequent visitor who loved to talk with me about Hinduism—but I was in no mood for that now. With long white hair and beard, and dressed in a saffron dhoti, the old gentleman was the very image of the classical Hindu holy man, a role he played to the hilt with appropriate theatrics, although he was a sincere Hindu, too. I waved back and watched with a smile as he climbed the steps, hitting each one sharply with the impressive walking stick he carried more for effect than necessity. Govinda, as usual, was singing in Hindi at the top of his voice when he disappeared into the house.

Why I Am Not a Christian had turned out to be a disappointment. I had gotten it from the school library, hoping it would help me to remain a Hindu. But Russell's arguments were weak and contrived, and the more I read of why he had not become a Christian, the more convinced I became that I *must* become one—the evidence demanded it. I laid the book down and looked up into the sky with its scattered white clouds, resting my eyes, and thought deeply. How much longer could I refuse to receive Christ when I knew that he was in fact the true God, the Savior who had died for my sins? I was miserable, held back by the fear of losing my position in the Hindu community and the goodwill of my family. But wasn't Truth—and my relationship to God—more important? Yes, but I was still afraid.

My cousin Krishna came out onto the veranda. "Oh, there you are, Rabi. I've been looking for you. There's a meeting in Couva tonight that you ought to go to." He sounded very excited.

"What's it about?"

"It's a small Christian meeting. They'll be explaining the Bible."

Krishna had seemed so different lately, so joyful and easy to get along with. And now he was inviting me to a *Christian* meeting. Did he suspect what was going on inside of me? How I wanted to go! But what if the wrong people saw me there and rumors got started?

"How about it, Rabi? It would be really nice if you could come. I'm leaving at six thirty."

"Why not?" I said, surprising myself. "Yes, why not!"

On our walk to Couva, Krishna and I were joined by Ramkair, a new acquaintance of his. I had seen him around town, and he apparently knew much about me. "Do you know anything about this meeting?" I asked him, anxious to get some advance information.

"A little," he replied. "I became a Christian recently."

"A Christian?" I couldn't believe my ears. "Tell me," I said eagerly. "Did Jesus really change your life?"

Ramkair smiled broadly. "He sure did! *Everything* is different."

"Do you *know* God?" I asked.

"Yes, since I asked Jesus to come into my heart."

"It's really true, Rab!" added Krishna enthusiastically. "I've become a Christian, too—just a few days ago." That was the first time he'd ever called me Rab, like my closest friends did.

"I thought so!" I exclaimed. To my surprise, I realized that I was happy for him. Then my happiness turned to panic. What was happening to Hindus these days? Molli, Ramkair, and now Krishna! I'd never heard of anything like this in my life! Was I next?

After an hour's walk we reached the outskirts of Couva and turned onto a short, narrow side street in a very poor neighborhood. Asphalt from Trinidad's famous Pitch Lake has been used to pave streets in nearly every major country of the world, but none of it had gotten here in many years. What little blacktop remained was full of cracks and holes with grass growing through. There were only three structures on the street, and my attention was immediately caught by the poorest one of all, a ramshackle hall, badly in need of repairs and surrounded by high weeds. The rough siding, topped by a rickety corrugated roof, showed no sign of ever having been painted, and the boards were gray and moldy with age. Faded lettering, barely visible, proclaimed, HEART AND HAND HALL, an echo from better days. There was no sign to indicate that a meeting was being held there, but it wasn't needed. Loud singing, somewhat off-key but exuberant, was pouring out of the open windows, leaving no doubt in our minds that this was the place.

Walking hesitantly up the few broken concrete steps, I could hardly contain my excitement. Once I stepped inside it was difficult to believe my eyes. There weren't more than a dozen people present, and the "orchestra" I thought I'd heard as we had approached was a very small girl of about six standing in front and banging a cheap tambourine. So few people—but what enthusiasm! I had never heard such singing. We hesitated just inside the door. My eyes took in the dusty floor, the large cobwebs sagging from the rafters, sleeping bats in clusters here and there under the open roof, the unpainted walls displaying a few ancient and illegible advertisements. The tiny group of Christians was anything but impressive: a few elderly East Indians and blacks and a handful of teenagers and young children.

Although I recognized no one, I was sure that everyone would immediately know me. I dreaded what would happen when they told their Hindu neighbors that I had come to a Christian meeting. There was no way to be inconspicuous among such a small audience. Deciding to be brave, I marched up the narrow aisle between the dusty, empty wooden benches, followed closely by Krishna and Ramkair. Out of the corner of my eye I could see heads turning, expressions of surprise, and people nudging one another, but I kept on to the very front bench. A short chorus was being sung over and over with great enthusiasm:

> All the way to Calvary he went for me,
> He went for me, he went for me.
> All the way to Calvary he went for me,
> He died to set me free.
> Although I had so many, many sins,
> Jesus took them all away and he pardoned me.
> All the way to Calvary he went for me,
> He died to set me free.

It was the first Christian song I had ever heard. "Calvary" was apparently where Jesus had died for the sins of the world, and for my sins, too. So it is a real place! I thought. And such feeling in their singing—they must love Jesus very much for dying for them!

The little girl smiled at us shyly as she continued to bang away with her tambourine. The small audience sang the words over and over again. It surprised me when I realized that the three of us were joining in loudly, caught up in the enthusiasm. It was not unusual to sing at Hindu ceremonies, but never with the joy and exuberance of these Christians.

The small song leader held up her tambourine. There was a momentary pause; then she hit her hand with it again and a new chorus had started. Over and over the words were repeated, and soon I had joined in once more. It was hard not to be enthusiastic if what this song said was true!

Wonderful, wonderful, Jesus is to me!
Counselor, mighty God, Prince of Peace is he.
Saving me, keeping me from all sin and shame.
Wonderful is my Redeemer, praise his Name!

No one had started to preach, but already I had learned so much. What a contrast between the relationship these Christians had with Jesus and the ritualistic appeasement of the gods at Hindu ceremonies! I had never heard anyone say that a Hindu god was "wonderful" or a "counselor." Certainly no one would sing like that about Shiva, about Kali, his bloodthirsty wife, or about their favorite son, Ganesha, half elephant and half human! And they called Jesus the Prince of Peace! No wonder Molli said she didn't need to do yoga anymore to achieve peace. The words of that simple chorus were burning themselves into my heart. Jesus would not only save, he would keep me from all sin and shame. What good news! These people must have found it to be true or they wouldn't be singing with such enthusiastic joy.

While we sang several choruses a few others came in, swelling the audience to about fifteen. At last the little girl sat down, and a young man I hadn't noticed when we came in walked to the front.

"We welcome all of you here this evening to our gospel meeting," he said with a smile. "Please turn in your hymn sheets to number ten." It was the last one on the sheet.

I could hardly believe my eyes. I remembered him as one of the worst rowdies from my primary school days—and a Muslim, at that—whom I had intensely disliked. How different he seemed now. And the hymn he had asked us to sing astounded me, especially the chorus:

Sunlight, sunlight, in my soul today;
Sunlight, sunlight, all along the way.
Since my Savior found me, took away my sin,
I have had the sunlight of his love within.

What a profound effect those simple words had upon me! Worshiping the sun up in the sky for an hour each day,

I had remained dark and cold inside. But these people were singing about sunlight *in their souls*. And it was a sunlight of love! I could hardly contain my wonder and excitement. *The sunlight of his love within.* Well, I didn't have any love to sing about. I hated so many people, in spite of my diligent practice of religion. I knew that most Hindu holy men nursed a great deal of resentment and hatred in their hearts. There was a lot of jealousy between the pundits, who often hated each other with a passion. Certainly Hindus hated the Muslims and had slaughtered scores of thousands of them in India just after Independence. But these Christians were singing about Jesus' love being *in* them, a love so pure and bright and real—not just an idea—that they described it as being like *sunlight in their souls.* Well, I wanted to have that love in my soul, too!

After a few more hymns, the preacher, Abdul Hamid, came to the front and an offering plate was passed around. I dropped in a penny and heard a few more coins falling in as the plate moved through the small audience. How pitiful, I thought, compared to the huge offerings I've gathered at *pujas.* The preacher will be indignant!

How mistaken I was! When those few coins were brought up to him, Abdul Hamid closed his eyes and began to pray: "We thank you, heavenly Father, with our whole hearts for this blessing we receive gratefully from you. Help us to use it prayerfully and carefully in your service and to your glory. In Jesus' name we pray. Amen."

I almost laughed at the thought of using those few coins "prayerfully and carefully." What pundit would ever think of using a *puja* offering or any of his fees to the glory of Hanuman or any other god? He would do whatever he wanted with it. How greedy and selfish I had been with the offerings laid at my feet! Ramkair whispered to me and Krishna that the preacher, who had a wife and three children, had given up his teaching position and a good salary to be an unpaid evangelist. It was more than I could comprehend.

Taken from Psalm 23, the sermon was very simple yet

profound. It was delivered with deep conviction and a spiritual power that I had never experienced before. Every word seemed to be directed at me. I wondered how this man knew my inner struggles, the questions that had bothered me, the very thoughts I had been thinking, the deep conflicts I had experienced. Surely he hadn't known I was coming!

"The Lord is my Shepherd; I shall not want." Something within me leaped at those words. An inner voice seemed to be calling me to let the true God be my Shepherd. But another voice fought and argued against all the preacher said. It warned me that I would lose everything and reminded me of the prestige and honor I could have as a great pundit like Jankhi Prasad Sharma Maharaj. My mother's heart would be broken! How could I bring disgrace upon my father's good name? The two voices argued, but the voice drawing me to the Good Shepherd spoke with love, while the other voice spoke with hatred and threats. Truly this Shepherd the psalmist described was the God I had been searching for! Even if I lost everything else, what would it matter? If I let the Creator become my Shepherd, then what else could I want? If he was mighty enough to create the whole universe, surely he could care for me.

"He leadeth me in the paths of righteousness for his name's sake." How guilty I felt, and how futile all my efforts had been to make myself morally clean! After thousands of holy baths, I was still sinful on the inside. But this God promised to lead me into righteousness, not so that I could boast of my own goodness, or improve my karma so I could have a better reincarnation; he would forgive me so that I could belong to him, even though I didn't deserve it, and then he would help me to live the life he had planned for me. It would be *his* righteousness, given to me as a gift, if I would receive it. Slowly the wonder of God's grace, so unlike anything I had ever heard, became believable.

"Yea, though I walk through the valley of the shadow of death, I will fear no evil: for thou art with me." In spite of the old English this was plain enough. I would be set free from the fears I had lived with all of my life—fear of the spirits that haunted our family, fear of the evil forces exerting their influence in my life, fear of what Shiva and the other gods would do if I didn't constantly appease them. If this God was my Shepherd, I need have no fear because he would be with me, protecting me, giving me his peace.

"Surely goodness and mercy shall follow me all the days of my life: and I will dwell in the house of the Lord for ever." The preacher said that meant being in heaven in the presence of God. Well, that was far better than Self-realization!

"The Lord Jesus Christ wants to be your Shepherd. Have you heard his voice speaking to your heart? After his resurrection Jesus said, 'Behold, I stand at the door and knock' —this is the door of your heart—'if any man hear my voice, and open the door, I will come in to him, and will sup with him.' Why not open your heart to him now? Don't wait until tomorrow—that may be too late!" The preacher seemed to be speaking directly to me. I could delay no longer!

Jumping up from my seat, I went quickly and knelt in front of him. He smiled at me and asked if anyone else wanted to receive Jesus. No one stirred. Then he asked the Christians to come forward and pray with me. Several did, kneeling beside me. For years Hindus had bowed before me— and now I was kneeling before a Christian.

"You're not coming to me," he said, "but to Jesus. He is the only one who can forgive you and cleanse you and change your life and bring you into a living relationship with the living God." I understood that without any explanation. I was kneeling there to let him show me how to receive this Jesus he had been talking about.

Aloud I repeated after him a prayer inviting Jesus into my heart—except for the words "and make me a Christian." I wanted Jesus, but not *that*. I didn't yet understand that inviting Jesus into my heart made me a Christian and that no one can become a real Christian in any other way.

When Mr. Hamid said, "Amen," he suggested that I might want to pray in my own words. Quietly, choking with emotion, I began. "Lord Jesus, I've never studied the Bible and don't know what it's all about, but I've heard that you died for my sins at Calvary so I could be forgiven and reconciled to God. Please, Lord, forgive me all my sins. Come into my heart! I want to be a new and changed person!"

I wept tears of repentance for the way I had lived: for the anger and hatred and selfishness and pride, for the idols I had served, for accepting the worship that belonged to God alone, and for imagining that *he* was like a cow or a star or a man. I prayed for several minutes—and before I finished I knew that Jesus wasn't just another one of several million gods. He was in fact the God for whom I had hungered. I had met Jesus by faith and discovered that he himself was the Creator. Yet he loved me enough to become a man for my sake and to die for my sins. With that realization, tons of darkness seemed to lift and a brilliant light flooded my soul. The "sunlight of his love" had come to shine in my heart, too!

Astral travel to other planets, unearthly music and psychedelic colors, yogic visions and higher states of consciousness in deep meditation—all these things, once so thrilling and self-exalting, had become dust and ashes. What I was experiencing now was not just another psychic trip. I was sure of that. Molli had said that Jesus would prove himself. At last I knew what she had meant. He had come to live in me. I knew he had taken my sins away. I knew he had made me a new person on the inside. Never had I been so genuinely happy. Tears of repentance turned to tears of joy. For the first time in my life I knew what real peace was. That wretched, unhappy, miserable feeling left me. I was in communion with God and knew it. I was one of God's children now. I had been born again.

The small congregation began to sing, "Just as I am, without one plea, but that thy blood was shed for me; and that thou bidst me come to thee, Oh, Lamb of God I come,

I come." I stayed on my knees listening to each word, filled with gratitude to God for his forgiveness, amazed that this song expressed exactly the way I felt. The writer must have experienced this same release from guilt. From that word "Lamb" I understood immediately that Jesus was gentle, kind, and loving. I remembered what Molli had said about the love of Jesus. I felt that love flooding my soul.

All my pride in being a Brahmin had vanished. It had taken a lot of humility for a high-caste Hindu to kneel down on that dirty floor in front of those Christians, but that was just the beginning of a new realization of how small I was and how great was my God. I discovered that humility wasn't demeaning and didn't cause me to hate or look down upon myself. It was simply admitting the truth that I was completely dependent upon my Creator for everything. That confession opened the door to a whole new life in Jesus.

With tears of joy and happy smiles, the small congregation crowded around to hug me and shake my hand as though they were welcoming me into God's family. I had never felt such joy and love from other human beings or such a sense of belonging, not even among my own relatives. Imagine my joy when Shanti came up and embraced me. I hadn't known she was there. "I came in a friend's car," she whispered. "Rab, I'm really happy you've given yourself to Jesus. It's the best thing you've ever done!" I sensed a new relationship between us. She was in God's family, too!

On the way home, the tall cane pressing in on each side of the road, leaves shimmering in the pale moonlight, seemed almost to dance in the ocean breeze. And the stars! I could not remember their being so bright! I had always loved nature, but now it seemed ten times more beautiful than ever before. Once I had worshiped the heavenly bodies, but now I saw them in a different light. They had been made by this God whom I had just come to know, and I reveled in appreciation of the Creator's power, artistry, and wisdom. I just wanted to worship him forever, to tell him how grateful I was for life itself. Now I no longer wished I had never been born. I was happy to be alive—and alive forever! The three of us had a joyous time as we walked, singing over and over the choruses we had learned that night.

Arriving home at last, Krishna and I found the entire family—except Deonarine and his wife—gathered in the sitting room waiting up for us, apparently having heard what had happened from Shanti, who had already arrived by car. I had been afraid of being seen at that meeting, but all fear had left me when Jesus came into my heart. I couldn't keep such good news to myself. I wanted everyone to know my Lord.

"I asked Jesus into my life tonight!" I exclaimed happily, as I looked from one to another of those startled faces. "It's glorious. I can't tell you how much he means to me already. I know he's made a new person out of me."

"I couldn't believe it, Rabi, but now I've heard it from *you*," said Aunt Revati in a choked voice. "What is your mother going to say about this? She'll be shocked." She walked abruptly from the room, but without the display of anger I had expected. Instead she seemed wounded and bewildered.

How sorry I was that Aunt Revati hadn't given me a chance to explain. I had a new love for her and wanted her to know the peace I had found. And Ma—what would be her reaction? I looked over at her, and to my surprise I saw that she was beaming.

"You've done the best thing, Rabi!" she exclaimed happily. "I want to follow Jesus, too!"

I ran to Ma and put my arms around her. "I'm sorry for the way I've acted—please forgive me!" She nodded, too overcome to speak.

Shanti was crying now. "I gave my heart to Jesus, too, a few days ago," she managed to say between sobs of joy, wiping at her tears.

We sat talking excitedly for a long time, sharing the new love we had for one another in Christ. Ma told me how Shanti had slipped away to that meeting in Couva a few nights before and had been caught by Aunt Revati climbing in a window when she came home. Uncle Deonarine had given her a good thrashing. I told Ma about the sermon, and she said that Psalm 23 had been her favorite and that she had read many of the Psalms before Nana had destroyed her Bibles. At last, reluctantly, we said our good nights.

Before going to bed I destroyed my secret cache of cigarettes. All desire for them had left me. At my first opportunity the next day, I apologized to Aunt Revati for the way I had so often treated her. She didn't know how to react. This was not the Rabi she had known for so many years. I could see the uncertainty in her eyes and felt sorry for her. She looked so miserable. How well I understood the struggle going on in her heart.

Uncle Deonarine was out in front polishing his car—the one I had blessed—when I found him. It was not easy to face him, and I hesitated to say bluntly that I was a Christian. I walked over to him and said, "Uncle Deonarine, I've received the Holy Spirit into my life."

He straightened up and looked at me with astonishment and anger. "Your father was a great Hindu and your mother is a great Hindu," he said sternly. "She would be most displeased to think you were becoming a Christian. You'd better think twice about what you're doing!"

"Yes, I have already counted the cost," I replied.

Krishna was able to talk to his mother as none of the rest of us could, and he discovered that she had been disillusioned with her religious rituals for years but was afraid to show it. He gave her the address of a church in a nearby town, and the following Sunday she went there alone, though hesitantly. When she returned late that evening, those of us who had already become Christians were waiting up for her, believing that our prayers had been answered. No one needed to ask what had happened—the expression on her face told it all.

She and Ma hugged each other and cried and cried. Then Aunt Revati straightened up, wiped her eyes, and looked at me. "Rabi!" We held one another in a long embrace, tears running down our cheeks, the hatred and bitterness between us gone forever.

The following day I walked resolutely into the prayer room with Krishna. Together we began to carry everything out into the yard: the Shiva lingam and the other idols of wood and clay and brass that we had called gods; the Hindu scriptures, volumes of them, wrapped in their sacred cloths; all manner of religious paraphernalia used in the ceremonies. Until Aunt Revati had become a Christian, too, I had not felt free to do this. Now we were all united in the one desire to rid ourselves of every tie with the past and with the powers of darkness that had blinded and enslaved us for so long. Others joined us, and together we carried out the huge altar. When the prayer room was completely empty, we swept it clean. Going carefully through the house, we searched out every charm, amulet, fetish, religious picture, and artifact, throwing them all on the rubbish heap behind the garden. Uncle Deonarine and his wife were aghast but made no attempt to stop us. Everyone else was in accord. Altogether, thirteen of us had opened our hearts to Christ and knew that our sins were forgiven—ten in our own household and three other cousins.

Joyful in our new freedom from the fear that had once bound us, Krishna and I smashed the idols and religious pictures, including those of Shiva. A few days earlier I wouldn't have dared even to think of doing that, fearful of being killed by the Destroyer immediately, but the iron grip of terror that had held me for so long had been broken by the power of Jesus. No one had told us what to do. Our eyes had been opened by the Lord. We knew that there was no compromise, no possible blending of Hinduism and true Christianity. They were diametrically opposed. One was darkness, the other light. One represented the many roads that all lead to the same destruction; the other was, as Jesus had said, the narrow road to eternal life.

When everything had been piled on the rubbish heap,

we set it on fire and watched the flames consume our past. The tiny figures we had once feared as gods were soon turning to ashes. The evil powers could terrorize us no longer. We hugged one another and offered thanks to the Son of God who had died in order to set us free. As we sang and prayed and praised the true God together, we could see that new freedom and joy shining in each other's faces. What an unforgettable day!

Pushing the dying embers together, determined to see the past consumed, I found my thoughts going back to my father's cremation nearly eight years before. In contrast to our newfound joy, that scene had aroused wailing cries of inconsolable grief as my father's body had been offered to the very same false gods who now lay in smoldering fragments before me. I thought of the intervening years and of my resolve to be just like my father. It seemed unbelievable that I should be participating with great joy in the utter destruction of that which represented all I had once believed in so fanatically. Indeed, all that I had lived for was going up in flames—and I praised God!

In a sense this was my cremation ceremony—the end of the person I had once been . . . the death of a guru. In the few days since my spiritual rebirth, I had begun to understand that being "born again" really involved—through Christ's death and resurrection for me—the death of my old self and the resurrection of a new person.

The old Rabi Maharaj had died in Christ. And out of that grave a new Rabi had risen in whom Christ was now living.

How wonderfully different from reincarnation was resurrection. The slate was wiped clean, and I eagerly looked forward to my new life in Jesus, my Lord.

FIFTEEN

A New Beginning

What a transformation had taken place in our family! Instead of quarreling and bitterness, we now had harmony and joy. The difference Christ had made was so great that it caused daily astonishment to each of us. The hatred that had burned for years between me and my aunt seemed like a nightmare from which we had both awakened. The religion we had once practiced so zealously had actually increased the antagonism between us—in the midst of a family *puja* Aunt Revati had once even thrown a brass lota filled with holy water at me. But Christ had changed us both. Now we loved one another very much. She was like a mother to me once again, but in a new way, and her son, Krishna, whom I had also hated, was closer to me than a brother. Indeed, we were brothers in Christ. The past was gone, consumed as surely as the idols that had been burned to ashes on the rubbish heap.

God's grace had made the difference. As Hindus we had no concept of forgiveness, because there is no forgiveness in karma, and therefore we could not forgive one another. But because God had forgiven us through Christ, we could also forgive each other. We learned that Christ had taught that those who would not forgive others from their hearts would not be forgiven by the Father. But he had put that spirit of forgiving love in our hearts, and I could never again hold a grudge against anyone. Words that we had not been able to speak with sincerity before—"I'm sorry" and "I for-

143

give you"—were now heard in our home whenever they were needed, and therefore the joy in our hearts was able to grow.

Miracle of miracles, I began actually to take delight in helping around the house. We teenagers all pitched in and pulled weeds, watered plants, cultivated flower beds, and raked leaves. Under the wondering gaze of the neighbors the yard took on a new look. No one could miss that transformation!

There was another change that was not visible from the outside, but which meant even more to us. The haunting footsteps of Nana were no longer heard storming up and down the attic or stamping outside our bedrooms at night. The peculiarly disagreeable odor that had often accompanied these phenomena and that we had never been able to trace had disappeared, never to return. And no longer were objects suddenly moved by some invisible force off the sink or a table or out of a cupboard to crash to the floor. We understood at last that the cause of all of these things had not been Nana's spirit, as we had supposed, but spirit beings the Bible called "demons"—angels who had rebelled with Satan against God and were trying to confuse and to deceive men into joining their rebellion. They were the real power behind the idols and every philosophy that denied the true God his rightful place as Creator and Lord. I now understood that these were the beings I had met in yogic trance and deep meditation, masquerading as Shiva or some other Hindu deity.

Reading the New Testament, the pieces of the puzzle —who I was, why I existed, and the destiny God had planned for me—began to fall into place and an orderly answer to so many questions took shape. On my knees I would ask God to reveal the meaning of Scripture; then I would read each verse slowly, digesting it and trusting the Holy Spirit to give me understanding. I spent hours each day in prayer and reading God's Word—hours that I once had given to the worship of the sun, the cow, the helpless idols on the altar, and to yoga and meditation. In this careful way I read through the New Testament again and again. I read the Old Testament, too, and discovered that the Bible was not a book of mystical, vague, and contradictory "ancient wisdom" or myths about make-believe characters like Rama and Krishna who never existed. It was historical—about real people like Abraham, Daniel, Peter, and Paul, who came to know God, and about real nations like Israel, Egypt, Greece, and Rome. I saw that God, the Creator, had a purpose for all men. He was the God of history and he was still working in the lives of men and the affairs of nations. The Bible also revealed what God was yet to do in bringing history to its climax—and I began to see current events, especially the fulfillment of prophecy unfolding in the Middle East, in a new light. Our family had some exciting times as we began to share with each other what we were learning from God's Word.

Ma read the Bible with a simple, childlike faith. If this Holy Book inspired by God made a promise to her, Ma believed it and acted upon it. It was that simple. Jesus had healed the sick, and Ma could see no reason why he wouldn't also heal her. "You are so real to me, Lord!" she told him. "Long ago you did these wonderful miracles, and you are still alive today. I would like to walk again. Thank you, Lord." She was sure he would heal her.

Gradually the miracle took place. Daily we saw an improvement. She grew stronger, began to stand a little, then to take hesitant steps holding onto furniture. Within a few weeks she was moving around in the kitchen, helping to prepare the meals, and soon after that she could climb up and down the stairs outside and walk around in the yard to get a closer look at the birds and flowers she had always admired from her window. "Praise the Lord!" she exclaimed again and again. "What the best medical experts and highest-paid Hindu healers could not do, Jesus, who is still alive today, has done!"

Before her healing, Ma could not kneel at all. But kneecaps that seemed to have dissolved over the years were miraculously restored, and now she began to spend at least five hours a day on her knees in prayer. She seemed to have a special ministry of intercession, praying for the rest of the family, for our neighbors, and for relatives, that they might know Christ and have fellowship with the living God. Although she was over seventy years of age, Ma would rise at about 6 A.M., and at 11 A.M. she would still be on her knees in prayer, having taken no time out for breakfast. When at last she emerged from her room, there was a glow on her face and everyone knew that she had been with Jesus.

Rumors spread swiftly through our town and beyond. At first few could believe that we had really become Christians. It was far easier to imagine that we had all gone mad. Visitors came in a steady stream to check out the rumors for themselves. Some argued heatedly. Others seemed too stunned to say much, after hearing the story from our own lips, and left in a state of shock. But surprise and shock soon turned to active hatred and opposition. Those who had once bowed before me and addressed me reverently now sneered when they saw me and shouted nasty names. They were outraged that we had destroyed our idols. We tried, in a kind way, to explain the impotence of these false gods to help us, and to tell them of the true God who had come as a man to die for our sins. At first neighbors and relatives steadfastly refused to accept the forgiveness God offers through Christ. I understood exactly how they felt. Nothing could persuade them until truth meant more to them than tradition.

Through Molli's investigation we learned that there was a small group of Christians meeting in our own town. The following Sunday I set out joyfully on the short walk to this tiny fellowship that met under a house that was raised on stilts just high enough to provide a low-ceilinged shelter from the blazing sun and sudden rainsqualls.

"All-you, come and see Jesus Christ heself! Look, he passin' by!" a neighbor woman yelled as I walked past.

"I'm not Jesus Christ," I replied with a smile, "but I'm glad to be one of his followers."

The little church that met under the house was made up of a mere handful of Christians: a few low-caste East Indian families and several blacks, none of whom I would have associated with as a Hindu. But what a warm welcome they gave us! How strange it seemed, and yet how wonderful, to throw my arms around those whom I had once despised and even hated. Now I loved them with the love of Christ my Lord and embraced them as brothers and sisters. I had been delivered from the caste distinctions that lie at the very heart of the religion I had so zealously practiced and that cannot be eradicated from the Hindu mind. Following logically from karma and reincarnation, caste provides the many levels through which one must climb in one's upward evolution to God. The higher states of consciousness sought in meditation are subtle extensions of the caste system. Once it had seemed so divine, but now I saw caste as a great evil that erected cruel barriers between human beings, giving to some a mythical superiority while condemning others to be despised and isolated.

During the Christmas vacation, my father's brother, Nandi, invited me to spend some time with his family, where I had spent so many happy holidays. As soon as I arrived he lost no time in beginning to reason with me very earnestly

"Well, Rabi, I have heard some strange things about you. You know full well the life your father lived. He set the very highest Hindu standard. Your mother is also a most holy woman and extremely devoted to our great religion." In his mind I was still a Hindu.

I nodded solemnly, appreciating his concern for me. Did he remember how upset I had been to learn that he ate meat? Since becoming a Christian I had found my new diet, which now included eggs and a small amount of meat, beneficial. I had been very sickly before, suffering from a lack of protein.

For my uncle, however, to eat meat was to deny one of the most important tenets of his religion—that unity of all things that gives sacredness even to the lowest forms of life. To eat an animal was like eating a human. He was chiding me for turning away from the religion he didn't fully follow himself.

"You know," he continued, "that Hindus for miles around look up to our family. Everyone knows how faithfully you have observed our dietary laws. You can't afford to make a mistake like this and lose everything you have worked so hard for!"

"But I believe that Jesus is the only true God, the Savior, who died for our sins." I spoke softly and respectfully, wishing so much not to offend him. I loved him very much.

Reverently Uncle Nandi took the *Bhagavad-Gita* down from its high shelf and unwrapped it carefully from its saffron cloth. "Listen to what Krishna says in chapter four: 'Whenever there is decay of righteousness . . . then I myself come forth; for the protection of the good, for the destruction of sinners, I am born from age to age.'" He read the words slowly, watching my reaction closely.

"It is clear that Krishna came back once as Jesus," he continued. "Every Hindu who knows about him believes that Jesus is one of the gods. You don't have to become a Christian because you believe that Jesus is a god. That is for people who were born Christians—but you were born a Hindu. Whatever you believe, don't change your religion. You must always remain a Hindu."

"Well, I can't agree with that," I said firmly but politely. "Jesus said that he is *the* way, not *a* way; so that eliminates Krishna and everyone else. He did not come to *destroy* sinners —like Krishna said of himself—but to *save* them. And no one else could. Jesus is not just one of many gods. He is the only true God, and he came to this earth as a man, not just to show us how to live but to die for our sins. Krishna never did that. And Jesus was resurrected, which never happened to Krishna or Rama or Shiva—in fact, they never existed. Furthermore, I don't believe in reincarnation, because the Bible says that 'it is appointed unto men once to die, but after this the judgment.'"

My aunt was listening sadly, barely able to restrain herself from crying. Uncle Nandi looked so disappointed. He was a very sincere and kind man. I respected him very much. But there was no way to get him to consider the evidence and to look at Hinduism logically or to admit its inconsistencies. His great concern was that I must not violate a tradition that I had been born into. He would not care if I added Jesus to my list of gods, or even if I were an atheist who believed in no gods—just so long as I still called myself a Hindu. But to me it was a matter of truth, not tradition. After about an hour it became clear that further discussion was useless. By mutual consent I returned home that same day.

Gosine could not accept the fact that I had become a Christian. Like Nandi, he also believed that Jesus was just one more god among millions, another way that would eventually lead to Brahman. "What I go tell you, *Bhai!*" he said to me more than once. "All de roads do lead to de same place!" I tried to reason with him, to explain that I was not going to the "same place" he was. Jesus had told the Jews to believe in him; otherwise "ye shall die in your sins: whither I go ye cannot come." But it was no use. Gosine was not going to change his beliefs, no matter what evidence I presented. We could no longer communicate, and it saddened me very much.

Of course it was inevitable that our dear friend Pundit Jankhi Prasad Sharma Maharaj should drop in to check out the rumors and to try to persuade us to give up this madness called Christianity. Glancing around as soon as he entered, Baba noticed sadly that the pantheon of Hindu deities which had hung for years in numerous pictures on our walls was missing. He eased himself into the chair we offered, took a deep breath, and let out a long sigh.

"I cannot understand it," he began sadly. "Why should people tell these lies about you? They have said that you are all Christians now." Tears came to Baba's eyes. "I don't believe it!" he declared vehemently. "Tell me it isn't true!" Deep concern was written on the face of this gracious old man whom we all loved so much.

"But it *is* true, Baba," said Aunt Revati in Hindi.

He turned to me, such sorrow in his eyes. "Your father —what would *he* think? And you, Rabindranath Ji . . . I don't believe it! Who has offended you? I know that sometimes the pundits are not all honest. Tell me what is the matter?"

"No one has offended us, Baba," I replied quickly. "We have discovered that Jesus is the Truth, and he has given us forgiveness and real peace. He loves you, too, and died for your sins. You, too, can find salvation in him."

How puzzled he looked, as though forgiveness was a concept that he found impossible to understand, as it had been for me. He seemed embarrassed, not knowing what to say. Looking over at Kumar, he asked in bewilderment, "And you too?"

Kumar had recently come home from England unannounced, surprising us most of all when he told us he had become a Christian.

"Baba," said Kumar respectfully, "you know very well that I was a hopeless alcoholic when I left Trinidad three years ago. There was nothing the Hindu gods could do for me. Karma could only drop me lower in my next reincarnation. You know, too, that many pundits are in the same condition and that practicing their religion doesn't help them. I had hoped to make a fresh start in London. Imagine my fears when a former drinking companion from Trinidad visited me there. The moment I saw him, however, I could see that he was a different person. He told me he'd become a Christian. 'Christ has set me free from alcohol,' he said. That sounded too good to be true. And besides, I wanted nothing to do with his religion. 'You were always a Christian,' I reminded him. But he explained to me that there are many people who call themselves Christians because they belong to a church, but they have never met Christ and are not really his followers.

"Well," continued Uncle Kumar, "now I was more afraid of his Christianity than I had been of his drinking, but I decided to be polite and show him around London. Since he is one of the greatest orators in Trinidad, I took him first of all to Speakers' Corner in Hyde Park. We were going from group to group listening when we came to a young man talking about Christ. Something told me that he was speaking the truth. I *knew* it, but I didn't want to listen. I drove back to my apartment, but I couldn't forget the things that my friend and this young man had said. I fell to my knees in my apartment and asked Christ to forgive my sins and to come into my heart as my Lord and Savior. I tell you gladly, Baba, that Jesus has given me complete peace and made me a new man. You remember how Ma used to complain to you about my drinking and how I squandered thousands of dollars on whiskey? Now I have no desire for alcohol."

Incredulous, Baba stared in wide-eyed wonder at his changed friend. Seeing that he was speechless, Aunt Revati leaned forward and spoke with great earnestness, looking into the old man's face.

"Baba, let me tell you what happened to me. I was in the prayer room doing my *puja* when a voice suddenly told me that all the gods I worshiped were false. Then the voice said, 'I am the way, the truth, and the life: no man cometh unto the Father, but by me.' I knew that was Jesus talking to me. A few days later I surrendered my life to him and he has made me into a new person. The past is gone, my sins are forgiven, and I know that I will be in heaven forever! Listen to what Jesus said: 'For God so loved the world, that he gave his only begotten Son, that whosoever believeth in him should not perish, but have everlasting life.' This salvation is for all castes and for the people of every nation. It is also for you. God will forgive you and give you eternal life, if you will only receive Christ into your heart and trust only in him."

Baba still seemed too stunned to speak. He looked from one to the other of us, knowing that he had lost his truest disciples. He stood up very slowly, an expression of bitter disappointment on his face. He was very polite, very kind, wanting to remain our friend, but we could see that he was trying to suppress an overwhelming emotion. There was a great sadness in our hearts as we said good-bye to him. We never saw Baba again.

The very people who had bragged about how broadminded Hindus were and who had claimed that Hinduism accepts all religions were the most bitter in denouncing us for becoming the followers of Christ. And the more we listened to those who tried to persuade us to return to the religion of our fathers, the more clearly we saw that loyalty to one's religion is seldom based upon a desire for truth but is usually an emotional attachment to cultural traditions. Many Hindus recite Sanskrit mantras all their lives without knowing what they mean. Most of the Hindus who came to argue didn't know why they were Hindus, except through birth, and had almost no grasp of many of the most basic elements of their religion. Our crime was that we had forsaken the religion of our forefathers—and that made any discussion about truth meaningless.

Oddly enough, many Muslims were just as resentful, even though it was not their religion we had left. One Muslim friend yelled at me angrily, "I hear you've begun to follow that crook Jesus!" Yet the Koran proclaims that Jesus lived a pure and sinless life.

It was hard, at first, to understand the anger and hatred that the name of Jesus stirred against us in the hearts of those who had formerly been our close friends. Later we read in the Gospels that Jesus had said that his followers would be hated by all men for his sake. Still, it was difficult to understand why anyone would hate Jesus, much less crucify him.

He had done nothing but good. But he claimed to be the *only* way to God, and we soon learned that this angered people because it meant they would have to give up their religious rituals and sacrifices and accept his death alone for their sins. This hatred for Jesus was turned against us, his disciples.

"You're a shame and disgrace to the Hindu community! Hypocrites! Traitors!" The loud voice startled me, and I ran out onto the front veranda to investigate. Krishna and Shanti were already there. A large American car was parked out on the road near our house. There was a loud-speaker on top and a man sitting in the back seat behind his chauffeur talking into a microphone. We recognized him—one of the richest men in Trinidad, a Brahmin and a Hindu leader.

"You've turned your backs on the religion and the gods of your ancestors. That's the worst thing any Hindu could ever do! You have given up the greatest dharma in the world! You will have to pay for this!" Apparently he had carefully prepared his speech, and he continued to read it in an angry voice for several minutes, no doubt encouraged to see our neighbors gathering in the street to listen. Then with a roar the car drove off toward the north.

It finally became too much for Uncle Deonarine and his wife. She had never really gotten along well with the other women in our household, even before the great change. And now that we had all become Christians, she and Deonarine found living under the same roof with us intolerable, so they moved out.

Taking the bus that distance to school every day was impractical. With Kumar's help, I found a place to stay with a family near Queen's Royal College. They were Hindus. The location was convenient, but the quarters were very crowded. There were two small bedrooms and ten of us in the house. The eldest son, who also attended high school, slept with me on the floor of the living room. It was very depressing to be surrounded by idols and pictures of Hindu deities again. These old friends had not yet heard that I had become a Christian. But when day after day I failed to attend the family *puja*, I had to explain.

"I've become a Christian," I said one evening.

The family stared at me with unbelieving eyes. The father began to laugh, thinking I was joking. But when he realized I was serious, the anger came. "You mean you've left the greatest religion in the world to become a Christian, of all things?" he said in a mocking tone. "Why have you done this?"

"I was searching for the truth, and I found that Jesus is the Truth, the only True God, who died for our sins."

They worked very hard to win me back. But attitudes changed when it became clear that I was serious about my choice. They would denounce me for being unfaithful to the religion of my ancestors, yet they were selling beef curry in their shop in front of the house—a clear violation of Hinduism. However, I didn't point that out. The father came home from work drunk nearly every evening. Now his curses, abusing the name of Jesus, were directed against me, and I was allowed no response. He was, however, a fairly decent man when sober, and in spite of the family's hatred of Christians they tried to be hospitable and kind in many ways.

Worse than human hostility was the increasing oppression I felt from demons, who were not inclined at all to kindness. I was surrounded by frightful-looking idols in that house. I knew the real power behind these leering masks and wondered whether I should have agreed to stay in such a home. There had seemed no alternative at the time.

Life had become very difficult again at school also. Having at last earned the respect of my classmates as a Hindu leader, now I was the butt of Jesus jokes. Even the boys I had thought were Christians were now attacking me. It all became so unbearable that one night, feeling the oppression of demonic powers as I lay on the living room floor, I couldn't go to sleep. "Lord," I cried softly, "why does it have to be so difficult to be one of your followers? I love you and have your peace in my heart, but this is almost more than I can bear at school and here in this house. Is this always going to be my lot?" I fell asleep at last, overcome with sorrow.

At about 2 A.M. I felt someone shaking me. Opening my eyes in surprise, I saw someone clothed in a bright white light standing beside me. Wide awake now, I sat straight up and looked at him. I knew it was Jesus, although he didn't look quite like any of the pictures I had seen. He held out his hand toward me and said softly, "Peace! My peace I give to you!" With those words he vanished, and the room became dark again. I sat there for a long time making sure that I was really awake. There was no doubt about it. I felt like shouting "Hallelujah!" For a long time I lay with hands under my head, looking up by faith into heaven, rejoicing in the Lord.

That experience gave me new courage. I had a new assurance that Christ would be with me, leading and guiding and caring for me. Of course I had believed that before and had been trusting him, but now I had a deeper confidence that the most difficult circumstances could not shake. That assurance has never left me and never will.

Imagine my excitement when one day I saw on the bulletin board at school a notice advertising a meeting of Youth for Christ to be held in the auditorium. It was the largest club in the school, yet I had never heard of it and had imagined that I was the only real Christian at Queen's Royal College. I was welcomed warmly at that first meeting I attended, and soon I had many Christian friends. My closest friendship developed with Brendan Bain, the son of a well-known umpire of cricket matches. He, too, had only recently become a Christian. Praying and studying the Bible together, we encouraged one another to live for Christ and to tell others about him. I was seeing friends won to Christ regularly now, through my own witness and also through the Youth for

Christ weekly meetings, where I had been invited to join the staff. It was not easy, however, to convince those "born" Christians that they needed to be born again.

To avoid confrontations with the Hindu family, I got permission to use a room very late at school. Much of the time I used for Bible study and prayer, and I often went back to the house when everyone was about to go to bed. When that building was demolished for new construction about a year later, I was forced to move. My new home was much more suitable, though farther from college, but Brendan let me use his bicycle for transportation, and my new landlady was a wonderful Christian who encouraged me in the faith.

As a young boy, out of curiosity I had taken my watch apart and put it back together numerous times. Now I put that knowledge to use, repairing friends' watches. My tools were a razor blade, a small penknife, and a pin. I would ride Brendan's bike into the center of Port of Spain each Friday evening to buy parts. Soon my reputation spread. Students and teachers were giving me their watches to repair, and I was earning enough for pocket money and to pay for part of my room and board.

On weekends I was able to get home to Lutchman Singh Junction, where I still taught a Sunday school class in the little church under the house. Krishna was now teaching in a government primary school in San Fernando. He and Shanti were both able to be home on weekends, too, so we had a good time studying the Word of God together and sharing what the Lord was doing in our lives. Ma was a great inspiration, especially in her prayer life. We loved each other dearly. She would spend time praying with me each weekend, asking the Lord to show me what he wanted me to do after graduation.

I had developed a desire to become a medical doctor. It appealed to me as a way to help people in need, and at the same time I would be able to share Christ with my patients. Perhaps I could even go to school in England.

SIXTEEN

Reunion and Farewell

"Rabi! Your mommy's coming home!"

Aunt Revati was standing in the veranda doorway, going through the day's mail while Ma looked on, excited by the sudden news that seemed impossible to believe. Could it be true—after eleven years?

"She wrote from London," my aunt said, passing along what she was gleaning from the letter. "She was getting a ship for Trinidad. Ai! It's *today* that she's arriving!"

Lari was home at the time on a brief visit from the United States, where he was working on his doctorate. Hearing our excited voices, he came hurriedly into the room. "What time does the ship dock?" he asked.

"It must already be there!" exclaimed my aunt. "We better hurry up!"

What a wild drive we had. The ship was at the dock when we arrived, and all the passengers had disembarked. My mother was nowhere to be seen. "She must have already taken a taxi!" suggested Lari at last. "Come on—let's hurry back to the house!" So back we went, this time driving even faster.

When we dashed up the stairs and all burst into the sitting room, there she was, the mother I hadn't seen since I was seven, standing near the dining room table, talking to Ma and looking a little bewildered, apparently surprised to see her mother still looking so young and walking now—although we had told her in our letters how the Lord had healed her.

Mother saw Lari, recognized him, and they embraced. Then it was Aunt Revati's turn. I was standing just inside the doorway watching the emotional scene, feeling sorry for my mother. I knew she must have walked through the house. The prayer room was empty. Gone were the gods and the pictures of the deities on the walls. It must have been a hard experience for her. Perhaps she was afraid to face us, a houseful of Christians and she still a devout Hindu. This was her house, her family, and yet we must have been strangers to her now.

She had been looking at me without any recognition in her eyes. Finally she said, "But where's Rab?"

No one said anything, and I too remained silent. "Who is that?" she asked, pointing at me. Still no one answered, waiting to see if she would recognize me.

The suspense was becoming unbearable. Aunt Revati said, "That's Rabi!"

Everyone had turned to look in my direction. Now I could restrain myself no longer. I ran to her and kissed her. She put an arm around me, but the warmth and emotion I had expected after eleven years wasn't there. We seemed to be meeting for the first time.

"How big you've grown, Rab! I wouldn't have recognized you." In spite of my love for her, I could sense a chasm between us.

"We must have just missed you," said Aunt Revati. "How long have you been here?"

"Not more than fifteen minutes. Don't worry about it."

"I'm so sorry!" said my aunt. "Coming all that distance after so many years, and no one at the dock to welcome you!"

"Oh, I know the mail isn't too reliable," replied my mother, wiping at her eyes. We all knew that her sadness was caused by something more important than not being met at the ship.

At last, after eleven years, here was the reunion that I had thought would never take place. We had so much to talk about. But there was a barrier between her and all of us that couldn't be denied. She was full of praise for Baba Muktananda, the guru in whose temple she had been living for so long. A qualified yoga instructor now, she wanted to talk about the benefits of body control and Eastern meditation—which we now knew opened one's mind to the domination of evil spirits, but how could we tell her that? There was so much she seemed to want to discuss with me about Hinduism—but she knew that I no longer agreed, and we both wanted to avoid an argument.

Philosophically it seems right to many to claim that Hinduism accepts all religions and that everyone is going to the same place, but by different roads. Those who plead for mutual tolerance and the syncretism of all religions fail to realize that there *are* grave differences which affect one's life. Such basic realities cannot be dismissed by ecumenical agreements. Mother was committed to the Hindu philosophy that there is only One Reality—Brahman—and that the law of karma demands future payment for past sins. The rest of us were convinced that good and evil are different, that the Creator is *not* the same as his creation, and we had come to know the forgiveness that Jesus brings and no longer believed in reincarnation. Between these opposite beliefs there was no possible meeting ground, no compromise without denying all meaning to language and ideas.

I knew it was very hard on my mother to face the fact that we were no longer Hindus. She seemed empty and uncertain in our presence. Everything had changed, except her; she was still committed to the old traditions based on a mythology we had rejected. After three days she went to Port of Spain to accept the highest position in the largest temple in Trinidad, which had been offered to her before she had left India. It hurt us all to see her go, especially so soon, but the barrier between us was very real.

"You must come and live with me in the temple!" she

urged me when she left. "As soon as you go back to school, come and see me! There are beautiful quarters for us to share together—and it's not far from Queen's Royal College!"

There was no possible way to persuade me to live in such a place, even to be near my dear mother, but I couldn't find the words to tell her. I dreaded even visiting her at the temple. I knew beyond the shadow of a doubt that those idols were only masks for demonic beings who kept the worshipers in chains of spiritual darkness. How well I remember that first visit! Someone showed me to her quarters. When I stepped through the door, Mother was seated in lotus position with clasped hands in front of a tall mirror, worshiping the Self. It broke my heart to see this. On one wall was a large picture of her guru, Muktananda, which she also worshiped several times a day.

She greeted me enthusiastically. "I'm so glad you could come, Rabi! Let me show you around." Taking me to the room adjacent to hers, she said, "Look! I've had this fixed up for you. When can you move in?"

"Well," I hedged, "this *is* quite a bit farther from school. . . ."

"Another five minutes is all." There was such disappointment in her eyes.

"I'll have to talk to the people I'm staying with."

Each time I came to see her the persuasions were renewed. I didn't know how to reply other than with vague and delaying answers. An outright refusal seemed cruel. How terribly difficult it must have been for her! She'd had such high ambitions for me to become a great Hindu leader. Instead, I was an embarrassment to her. She was revered by every Hindu on the island, and as she traveled about, lecturing, I knew that Hindu leaders asked her about me. Obviously I was a shame and a disgrace to her.

My real sorrow for her went much deeper, however, than her present pain. I feared for her eternal destiny. She was so devoted to false gods—but God, in his mercy, had reached me, and surely he could reveal himself to my mother. I prayed daily for her salvation. How much harder it would be for her than for most. Pride alone could blind her. It would be extremely difficult to give up the prestige she enjoyed and to incur the hatred and contempt of the Hindu community. Only once did I try to persuade her, referring to Jesus'statement, "I am the way, the truth, and the life."

"Of course I believe that!" Mother replied. "Jesus was saying that all of us are the way. The Vedas teach the same: that each person's dharma is different and each must find his own truth within."

"But Mommy! Jesus meant that he is the *only* way!"

After discussing this very briefly, we both realized that it wasn't profitable for us to have a religious argument, and we changed the subject. I knew from remarks she had made that she wasn't happy with herself, and I continued to pray that she would heed that inner hunger and seek the Lord.

"I'm going to be leaving in a few minutes for the television studios," my mother greeted me one afternoon when I had stopped in to see her. "I'm so glad you're here. Please come with me!"

I didn't want to go, knowing I would have to listen to one of her lectures on Hinduism and that she would expect me to comment afterward—which would only spark an argument. But I had no choice.

At the television station I watched as my mother sat in front of the camera and spoke of the value of yoga and meditation for bringing peace of mind. I was sure that she hadn't really achieved the peace of which she spoke. I knew from my own experience that I had tried to simulate peace, to make myself *feel* peaceful, but that it hadn't really worked. Peace comes only from a right relationship with one's Creator —a relationship she didn't yet have.

When the program came on the air, we watched it together. She turned to me when it was over. "What do you think of it, Rabi?"

How proud I would have been of my mother had I still

been a Hindu! But now her religious zeal and achievements only increased my sorrow. "You're a good speaker, Mommy," I said after hesitation, groping for words. "You have a good voice, and your television image comes over well."

The disappointment in her eyes told me that she had been hoping for more than that. Just avoiding an argument wasn't enough. Would she ever abandon the hope that I would turn back to Hinduism?

After my graduation, I began to be invited to speak at various churches around the island. Often Krishna came with me. We would give our testimonies and sing together, and we enjoyed every moment. Should I continue this life I loved or go on to the university? I often spent time in prayer with Ma and Aunt Revati, seeking God's will, and the increasing conviction grew on all of us that the Lord was leading me to England. I could think of no other reason than to go to medical school. As a doctor I could provide a service for humanity and at the same time tell my patients about Christ.

"Here's a letter for you from your Uncle Kumar," Aunt Revati told me one day as she went through the mail. He had returned to London a few months before my mother had arrived in Trinidad.

"He's inviting me to come to London to stay with him!" I exclaimed, growing excited as I read. I had just spent four days in prayer and fasting, seeking God's will, and this seemed to be confirmation that he was leading me to London, although I didn't have money for my fare. If it was God's will, he would provide the funds.

Early in February 1967, I heard of a ship, the S.S. *Antilles*, a large French liner, sailing for London on the fourteenth of that month. Deep within my heart I felt an assurance that I was to be on that ship, but days passed without any further confirmation in the way of funds. Nevertheless, on the morning of the twelfth when I could wait no longer, I went into Port of Spain and got a passport. Then I went immediately to the British High Commission for a visa.

"We can't issue a visa," I was told, "until you give us evidence that you are taking at least fifteen hundred dollars with you." And I didn't even have anything for my fare yet!

I left that office with only enough money in my pocket to pay for the ride back home. Arriving there that evening, I learned that three separate gifts had been given to me totaling exactly $1,500. Surprisingly, my mother was one of the donors. The fact that the gifts amounted to exactly the sum I needed—which I had told no one—was a further confirmation of God's guidance.

That evening another good friend offered to loan me the price of my fare. Here was another confirmation. The doors seemed to have definitely opened, with a place to stay in London and all the necessary money.

"I'm leaving for London on the fourteenth," I told the family that night.

"On the fourteenth? That's the day after tomorrow! How will you arrange it so quickly?"

"I got my passport today, and tomorrow I'm going to get my ticket and visa, God willing."

I didn't realize that getting a visa to England could be difficult. "I'm sorry, but we can't give you a visa," I was told sternly at the British High Commission the next day.

"But, sir, I have the fifteen hundred dollars that I'm required to take with me!"

"That doesn't mean you get your visa automatically."

"But why not?" I remembered hearing that the British government was becoming more restrictive about letting foreigners into the country.

He wouldn't explain. "I'm sorry, but I can't give it to you."

He had been thumbing through my passport and now laid it down on the counter between us. I didn't pick it up but looked past him out the window, praying silently. "Lord, please! Work this out!"

Picking up my passport again, he stamped the visa in it.

"Thank you, Lord!" I exclaimed under my breath.

Returning home that evening, visa and ticket in hand, I discovered that Ma and Aunt Revati had invited neighbors and relatives and friends for a farewell. My mother had come down from Port of Spain for the occasion. It was a very emotional time for all of us. My mother had only just come back, and now I was leaving. Ma was growing older and I hated to leave her. And Aunt Revati—how close we had grown in Christ, what real love God had given us for one another! And Shanti and Krishna—what good times we'd had together! And my other cousins who had become Christians, and aunts and uncles and cousins who had not . . . and my Uncle Deonarine, who had once been like a father to me but who hadn't come that night. . . . I didn't want to leave any of them. But I really believed that God had a plan and that he was leading me.

I listened to the speeches—well-meaning, loving, most of them very sincere. With tears in her eyes, Aunt Revati said that she loved me very much. She told how well we got along together and that she would miss my help around the house. That brought back memories of other days, and I praised God for the miraculous transformation he had made in each of us. Ma had similarly nice things to say, and even some of the Hindu neighbors told how they now respected me, having watched my new life carefully. Then my mother stood up.

"Rabi is my only child," she began, "and I certainly appreciate having a son like him!" I could hardly believe what she was saying. Tears were welling up in my eyes. "Since coming back to Trinidad, I have watched his life very carefully. I can only say that I am pleased with all that I've seen. In fact, I have been a secret admirer of his! As I've watched Rabi, there has been something special about him, a light that shines in his life."

It wasn't easy to hold the tears back. Knowing that my mother was a woman of few words made me appreciate what she had said all the more. I had never suspected that she had such thoughts about me, and I was moved deeply. It was an encouragement for me to continue to pray for her.

What she had seen was not my virtue or my light, but only the life and love of Christ in me through the new birth. Those were not my qualities that she had praised. Jesus had made the difference. He had changed me. And, oh, how I wanted my mother to enter into this new life in Christ, too!

SEVENTEEN

Where East Meets West

In London my life was to take a dramatic turn in a direction I would never have suspected. After it happened I could see how God had planned it all and prepared me. But before then tragedy struck our family back in Trinidad, and I regretted not being there to comfort Ma.

Shortly after I arrived in London, a cable came announcing the shocking and unexpected death of my Uncle Deonarine, who had once been like a father to me. Like Nana before him, he had died suddenly of a massive heart attack. Deonarine, however, had been stricken fatally much younger even than Nana, at the age of thirty-seven. Ma took it very hard.

Later we received news that was somewhat encouraging. Unknown to anyone else, Uncle Deonarine had held long and serious conversations about Christ with a young Hindu convert to Christianity. "Please pray for me," Deonarine had asked him more than once. We learned also that during a *puja* being said for him, my uncle had suddenly gotten up and left, leaving the pundit and everyone else dumbfounded— and he had refused to attend another *puja* after that. I earnestly hoped Uncle Deonarine had received the Savior before it had been too late. His sudden passing served to remind me of how short and uncertain life really is. I was glad that I had already surrendered my life to God, and I was trusting Him to do with me whatever he desired.

After working in a factory until the fall semester began, I entered a college recommended by Uncle Kumar for my premedical studies. The immorality among my fellow students appalled me. My stand for Christ was made known in a simple and unexpected way. The second or third day of school I found myself sitting in the front row in chemistry class. On my tie clasp large letters proclaimed *Jesus never fails*. In the middle of his lecture the instructor suddenly stopped and leaned forward to look at my tie clasp more closely. "Jesus never fails?" he read aloud in a mocking tone of mingled sarcasm and surprise. "Do you really believe *that?*"

Jumping to my feet, I said in a firm voice, "Yes, I believe it with my whole heart. Jesus has never failed me yet."

"Imagine that!" exclaimed the lecturer. Some of the students gasped audibly, and the expressions on their faces seemed to say, Is it really possible that we have someone in this class who believes the Bible? And he's an East Indian! The startling news swept through the school, and I became a marked man.

No sooner would I sit down at a table to begin eating lunch than fifteen or twenty students, often from several different countries, would bring chairs and sit around me. Immediately the questions would begin: Do you *really* believe in God? Why? What about evolution? Why do we need God any more; hasn't science explained everything? How can you believe in a resurrection? Why don't you believe in reincarnation? Some only wanted to heckle or argue, but many were seriously seeking Truth. Centering my answers upon the Word of God, I was prepared to discuss any subject from science to religion, politics, psychology—but my goal was always to win them to Christ. And some did recieve him.

Although busy with my studies and the growing Sunday school class I was teaching, I found time to go regularly to Hyde Park, Piccadilly Circus, and the Portobello Road to talk about Christ with anyone who would listen. In this way I began to encounter increasing numbers of drug addicts and made a startling discovery: some of them were having the same experiences on drugs that I had had in yoga and meditation! I listened in amazement as they described the "beautiful and peaceful world" they often entered through LSD, a world whose psychedelic sights and sounds were all too familiar to me. Of course many of them had bad trips on drugs, too, but most drug users seemed as reluctant to heed these obvious warnings as I had once been while practicing yoga.

"I didn't need drugs to have visions of other worlds and weird beings, and to see psychedelic colors and to sense a oneness with the universe and the feeling that I was God," I would tell them. "I got it all by transcendental meditation. But it was a lie, a trick of evil spirits who took over my mind when I relaxed control of it. You're being deceived. The only way to find the peace and fulfillment you seek is through Christ." The fact that I knew what they were talking about, and had experienced it all without drugs, caused many of these drug users to take seriously what I said.

Sometimes I visited an addict friend in his apartment to talk with him about Christ. One day when I arrived the door was ajar. When no one answered my insistent knock, I went inside. There was loud rock music blaring out of a speaker, psychedelic lights illuminating the room, and in the center of the floor, weaving around and making weird but to me familiar motions with his arms and body, was my friend.

"Pat!" I yelled, but he seemed as oblivious of my presence as my father had been for nearly eight years. "Pat!" I called loudly again and again, but it was impossible to get his attention. He was in another world on a drug trip just as I had often been, but through yoga.

Back in my own room I fell to my knees and cried to God for my friend. It had upset me very much to see that the motions he was making were exactly like those of the dancing girls in a Hindu temple. In fact Pat had become interested in Hinduism through his experiences on drugs. How it saddened me to see that he was selling his soul as well as ruining his body for experiences that I had discovered came from demons.

Another young addict used to visit some tenants in Uncle Kumar's apartment building where I lived. I loved to listen to this brilliant Cambridge graduate, a musical genius, play classics on the piano my uncle kept in a corridor. We had some long and serious discussions. Although Michael had never studied Hinduism or had any contact with Hindus—I particularly questioned him on that—his views of God, of the universe, and of human existence were precisely those that I had held as a Yogi. It astounded me to realize that through his experiences on drugs he had been won over to Hindu philosophy!

I began to ponder and to pray earnestly about the fact that so many addicts—though not all, by any means—had the same experiences as Yogis: what one got on drugs the other got through Eastern meditation. I learned that drugs caused altered states of consciousness similar to those experienced in meditation, making it possible for demons to manipulate the neurons in the brain and create all manner of seemingly real experiences that were actually deceptive tricks played on the mind. The same evil spirits that had led me ever deeper into meditation to gain control of me were obviously behind the drug movement, and for the same diabolical purpose. I began to see that the same satanic strategy lay behind drugs, meditation, free sex, and the rebelliousness of youth, expressed in the hippie movement that was just beginning in those days and embodied in certain music like that of the Beatles and the Rolling Stones. I remember a Rolling Stones concert where about 250,000 gathered in Hyde Park after the death of Bryan Jones from a drug overdose. They were as stoned on the music as they were on hash and LSD.

It startled me most of all to discover that the philosophy behind the whole counterculture of drugs, rebellion, and rock music was basically Hinduism: the same lies about the unity of all life, vegetarianism, evolving upward to union with the Universe, and doing one's own thing.* I discovered that young people by the thousands were not just dropping out to turn on with drugs, they were taking up transcendental meditation and various other forms of Yoga. Their whole way of thinking became clouded by Eastern mysticism. Nearly all began to accept reincarnation, which ended any belief in Christ's resurrection; the two are absolute opposites. Slowly and with a growing sense of alarm I became convinced that Satan was masterminding an invasion of the West with Eastern mysticism. I could see that few Christians really understood his plan and were prepared to combat it. Could it be that God was preparing *me*, an ex-Hindu, to sound a warning alarm to the millions in the West who were falling for an Eastern philosophy that I knew was false? I began to pray about that earnestly.

It was plain to see that God had a plan for my life, even though I didn't yet understand the new direction he would soon be leading me. It was wonderful to experience time and again God's provision for my needs, his unmistakable guidance and protection. The first Christian sermon I had ever heard had been about the Good Shepherd of Psalm 23; now he seemed intent upon showing me that I was one of his sheep and in his care.

One morning I had to get to class for exams but had no money for bus and subway fare. After praying about this need as I did about everything, I went to the bus stop as usual and stood in line. Just before the bus arrived, a woman came up to me and pressed a five-pound note into my hand, insisting that I accept it. I had won her husband to Christ some weeks earlier, and she was very grateful. However, I had given her no reason to suspect that I needed money. Only the Lord could have told her and brought her there at just that time.

---

* Hinduism teaches that each man's dharma, or rule of conduct, differs and must be discovered individually; there is no moral code binding upon all. Krishna taught that one can take any road—i.e., do one's own thing—and still get to him.

Another morning, as I was leaving for school, I felt impressed that I must go back into my room and pray for safety, which I did. Afterward, in line at the bus stop, I suddenly felt that I should get on a number 6 bus that was taking on passengers, although my number 52 bus was only a few seconds behind it. Without understanding why, I jumped aboard. The bus had just pulled away from the curb when I heard a horrible squealing of tires and looked back to see a car out of control plowing through that line of waiting people that I had just left. Jumping off, I tried to help. It was horrible. And I should have been one of the dead or dying. Although heartbroken for them, I was grateful to the Lord for having saved my life. Clearly he had a work for me to do. The next day the papers were full of the tragedy—there had been seven killed and six badly injured.

I listened to Billy Graham on the radio at every possible opportunity and found his messages challenging and helpful. Early in 1970, he began to announce a coming crusade for the city of Dortmund, Germany, that would be relayed on closed circuit television to large stadiums in thirty-nine cities—"from Amsterdam to Zagreb"—in eleven countries. Dr. Graham appealed to the Christians of Europe to unite in this great effort. As I prayed for God to provide the thousands of workers that would be needed, I felt a deepening conviction that praying was not enough. Should I quit school and go to Dortmund? That hardly seemed sensible. I was now in my third year, and looking forward eagerly to becoming a doctor.

Memories came back of those early and exciting days when I had newly become a Christian. From the very beginning I had wanted to tell the world about Christ. I had gotten on my knees while still in high school and cried, "Lord, let me preach the gospel to a million people!" It had seemed an impossible prayer because there hadn't been that many people in all of Trinidad, yet I had really believed that God would grant it. When Oswald J. Smith held meetings in Port of Spain, I had attended, remembering his name from that tract left beside my bed in the hospital. On the last night, he had called for all those who wanted to dedicate themselves to full-time Christian service to go into a prayer room. A few people, too old, it had seemed to me, to have many years left for the Lord, had responded.

"I believe there's a young man here that God is calling," Dr. Smith had said earnestly. "God wants to use him to win thousands to Christ. We'll wait another minute for him."

No one had moved. *Lord*, I had prayed fervently, *I don't know whether I'm that young man . . . but I'd like to be!* I stood up and went into the prayer room. When Dr. Smith had prayed with me I had really felt that I would become an evangelist. But I had been so young then. Now I was twenty-two.

Having heard Billy Graham's challenge, one memorable day in London as I prayed for God to supply the many workers that would be needed for the Dortmund crusade, I seemed to hear the Lord saying to me, Rabi, the time has now come! In my heart I responded, Yes, Lord!

That decision was to alter the whole course of my life, yet it had happened so quickly and so easily. I had learned to trust him, and my heart was at peace even though I didn't really know what lay before me. I only knew that the matter had been settled once and for all. I was not to be a doctor— and the pain I felt at giving that up was more than compensated by knowing that the Good Shepherd would lead me every step, though only one step at a time.

That very night, I had once again the same dream that the Lord had given me shortly after I had become a Christian. I was standing in a lush green field with Jesus beside me. Taking me by the hand, he led me up a grassy hill. When we reached the top, there were thousands of people on the other side looking up at us expectantly. Pointing to them, Jesus said to me, "Preach!" Awaking with that dream, now for the second time vividly impressed upon me, I felt that I had the confirmation I needed for such an important decision.

"I believe God wants me to go to Germany to help at

172

the Billy Graham meetings in Dortmund," I told Uncle Kumar later that morning. "I'll be leaving in a few days."

"But it's right in the middle of school!" he exclaimed incredulously. "How long will you be gone?"

How could I tell him I was giving up my plans to become a doctor, when he had been so enthusiastic about it? "I'm not sure," I said, hoping he wouldn't probe any deeper. He seemed satisfied. It would be easier to tell him everything later.

Having given away all my clothes and other possessions except for one change of clothing and a few books, I said good-bye to my uncle and London and the career I had expected to begin there. With a very small suitcase containing everything I now owned, and hardly enough money to last me a week, I set off on the train for Dortmund, not knowing a single word of German. Nor did I know anyone in all of Germany. I was like a little child setting out on a long journey and trusting all the details to his father.

Although I felt bewildered by the thousands of people all speaking a strange language hurrying along the crowded streets of Dortmund that first morning there, God graciously guided me right to the Graham Crusade office, though I didn't know the address. At the front door I was greeted in perfect English by a smiling German with extended hand who looked almost as though he'd been expecting me. "Good morning! Have you come all the way from India?"

"Just from London at the moment," I replied happily, "although I am an East Indian—from Trinidad."

"Where are you staying?"

"I was in a hotel last night . . ."

"Oh, we can't allow that! I'll see that you get settled. In the meanwhile we'll be having a good hot lunch soon."

He "settled" me in a beautiful home next to a large church, the Marienkirche. My hosts, the Klitschkes, couldn't have been more gracious. I soon forgot that I was a stranger in a strange land.

A reception for Billy Graham, attended by Christian leaders from all over Europe, was held in a hall adjoining the Klitschkes' home. Graciously I was invited, too. Among those well-dressed and prosperous Germans I felt quite out of place in my only suit, a cheap faded-brown one, made for the tropics, bought years before in Trinidad. But in spite of my appearance, the fact that I was the first ex-Hindu that most of these people had ever met made me an instant celebrity. Many invitations were extended to me to visit churches throughout Europe to tell the story of how I had come to Christ. This was heady stuff for a country boy from tiny Trinidad, especially when Dr. von Steiglitz, one of the organizers of the Dortmund meetings, introduced me to Billy Graham.

"Rabi, I preached the gospel in your country when you were a little boy," the great evangelist told me.

Those words ran through my mind for days. This man had preached the gospel in my country even before I had become a Christian, and he was still preaching it around the world. Would it be possible, in God's grace, that one day I, too, could preach the good news of Christ's love in many countries, especially in India? That seemed almost too much to hope for.

There in Dortmund, as in London, I seemed drawn to hippie drug users, and they to me. Many approached me with questions about the meaning of life, the existence of God, and seemed to think that because of my background in Hinduism I might be able to help them. From their lips I heard fresh evidence that LSD was often a ticket to an Eastern mind trip. Like the drug users I had met in England, the young people that I began to encounter in Germany had also adopted a Hinduistic philosophy of life. Yet they could see that it didn't answer their deepest questions, and they asked me to help them find the Truth.

Because of my own experiences in meditation, I could speak knowledgeably to drug users. However, I began to feel the need of some good theological training. I had always been against seminaries, because I thought they treated the Bible like a textbook instead of what I knew it to be, the Word of God that can only be revealed by the Holy Spirit. But I knew that I needed a systematic course of Bible study, and I began to ask God for guidance in this matter.

In the middle of his opening sermon the first night of those meetings, Billy Graham suddenly said, "I want to urge many of you young people to go to a good Bible college. Get a solid foundation to prepare you for the work God is calling you to do."

As though they had been spoken just for me, those words went like an arrow into my heart. Right where I sat I made a fresh dedication of my life to the Lord. Later, kneeling alone in my room, I prayed, *Lord, take me and use me. I cannot repay you for salvation, but I want to serve you. Prepare me to do something worthwhile that will affect thousands for eternity. Use me to the fullest extent possible.* The name London Bible College came to me clearly as I prayed, with the conviction that God wanted me to go there. The next day I wrote for an application form.

During those days in Dortmund I often heard of a young student from Brake Bible School in northern Germany that people said I *must* meet. "You two have the same vision and drive," they would say. Heinz Strupler was hearing the same thing about me. Eventually we met, but neither of us spoke the other's language, so we only spent a few brief minutes together at that time. Unknown to either of us, it was God's plan that we would be closely knit together in the service of the Lord in the years ahead. We would have been surprised to know where and how soon our paths would cross again.

EIGHTEEN

Dying We Live

Traveling through parts of Switzerland and Austria, visiting friends I had met at Dortmund, I found myself surrounded by beauty that far exceeded anything I had ever imagined. It was spring. At the lower elevations trees were sending out fresh shoots and the grass was turning green. Flowers of varieties and brilliant hues I had never seen were showing off their colors around the lakes and in the parks. And towering in silent majesty above this sprouting, blooming, singing paradise the ever-present Alps, still clothed in winter's icy shroud, made spring seem all the sweeter. Grateful to God, Creator and Master Artist, at times I felt I must burst with inexpressible joy at the sight.

Arriving in Zurich, drawn there by the stories I had heard about the many drug addicts who made it their Mecca, I found my way to an address that had been given to me in Dortmund. It turned out to be a home for the elderly at which meetings for hippies were held in the basement. When I arrived, an elderly but very dynamic man was leading a Bible discussion in German. After the meeting a young man welcomed me in English.

"I'm Martin Heddinger," he said with a friendly smile, glancing at my suitcase. "I hope you don't have anywhere to stay yet, because I'd like you to stay with my family."

"Will it be all right with your parents?" I asked.

"I'll call them to say you're coming. They'd love to have you live with us as long as you can."

The Heddingers turned out to be as kind and hospitable as the Klitschkes. What an enthusiastic welcome they gave me, a total stranger from a far land! I really felt Christ's love through them, and was soon calling Martin's parents Mamma and Daddy just as he did. They treated me like a son.

About two weeks after my arrival in Zurich, Heinz Strupler drove into town with four other Brake Bible School students and his fiancée, Annalies. They had also come to Zurich to work among the hippies. How happy I was to discover that Heinz shared my concern for these young people who were being swept into Eastern mysticism through drugs. He was also determined to recruit young Christians for world evangelism—and that, too, was one of my concerns.

"During the summers while in Bible school I've been working with Operation Mobilization," Heinz told me through an interpreter, gesturing forcefully as he spoke. "They organize young people around the world to preach in the streets and to go from door to door selling Bibles and Christian books and to help local churches evangelize their own countries. Now that I've graduated, I want to give my life to this task.

"It's a job for *everyone!*" he added in the thunderous voice he used when excited—which I soon learned was most of the time. Although he had a sharp sense of humor and could explode suddenly with laughter, Heinz's face always returned quickly to its usual serious expression that somehow seemed to fit his tousled blond hair and close-cropped beard. Seldom had I met anyone with such bubbling enthusiasm and burning zeal for Christ.

"I wasn't always like this," Heinz told me. "You know the Swiss. We're pretty hard to warm up or move. But when I became a Christian a few years ago Christ changed me completely—and I want the whole world to know what he can do." Here he slammed fist into open hand. "Yah, I really mean it! We've got to awaken the church right here in Switzerland. Most of the people who call themselves Christians have never been born again. Let me tell you, Europe is a real mission field. The church is stronger in Africa—there's a much higher percentage of Christians there—than in Germany or France or Austria."

Heinz was a great organizer, a man of action who wanted to get things done yesterday, not tomorrow. But he was not one to launch out in human strength and zeal without knowing the will of God and relying upon the power of the Holy Spirit. The seven of us spent a week in prayer and fasting seeking God's guidance. At the end of that time we were convinced that the Lord wanted us to establish an aggressive work among those elements of society that the churches in Zurich were largely ignoring. We all agreed to place ourselves under the leadership of Operation Mobilization as one of its teams. The only resources we had at the beginning, other than the love Christ had put in our hearts, were a small amount of pocket money and a broken-down Simca belonging to Annalies, who was as devoted to Christ as Heinz was.

We soon learned that it wasn't easy to recruit Christians, young or old, to work with Operation Mobilization. Few wanted to leave their comfortable homes and well-paying jobs. It was much easier to convince an ex-addict or converted prostitute to be a real disciple of Christ than it was to shake someone raised in the church out of his sleep. In fact, in those early days we had trouble getting into the churches. Some pastors thought we were trying to steal their young people, because many of those who had contact with us went off to Bible schools and missions. Most pastors, nevertheless, were eager to have me share briefly how I had turned from Hinduism to Christ—but few Christians wanted to hear anything that challenged their easy way of life. My story, however, always did just that.

From the very beginning in Zurich I found myself working day and night. During the day two or three of us would go into bars and hippie hangouts, trying to persuade these young people to give up their alcohol, drugs, and immorality, sharing with them the good news that Christ would give them the power to do it if they would receive him. We soon found ourselves in touch with prostitutes, homosexuals, and criminals because drug users often turned to these activities in order to support their habit. What joy it was to see ruined lives transformed by the power of God's Holy Spirit.

Each evening, when some of the young people we had met on the streets had gathered in that basement, I would share how and why I had become a Christian and the simple message of the gospel. Martin Heddinger was my interpreter. When the meeting had ended, we would sometimes shove the tables against the wall and let the hippies stretch out on the floor, for many had nowhere else to sleep. I often spent the night there, sometimes with thirty or more of them. It was a horrible experience of overpowering stench—some hadn't taken a bath in months—and madness as someone would suddenly have an LSD flashback and lose all control.

For many of these young people, Zurich was only a brief stop along the drug trail that would lead them through Turkey, Iran, Afghanistan, Pakistan, and finally to Goa beach in India. Some hoped to settle down in a Hindu temple to study under a guru; others were inclined toward Zen or other forms of Buddhism. The end result, however, would be the same: belief in reincarnation and the domination of their minds by evil spirits. Many would never return from their odyssey; they would die of overdoses and disease along the way. The paradise they hoped to find in India would turn out to be the very gateway to Hell!

I felt a great responsibility as night after night I shared how God had rescued me from the same satanic deception they were falling for. How I tried to persuade them to open their hearts to Christ! Some responded, others did not. But all seemed fascinated to hear how and why a religious Hindu had become a follower of Jesus the Messiah. I spent my days and nights talking with individuals, reasoning with them from the Bible and our common experiences, trying to explain that drugs and meditation only opened their minds to evil spirits;

the most beautiful experiences they would have on LSD or through meditation were the tricks of demons, enticing them to go deeper. But it was not easy to convince those who were already in the grip of clever deception.

There were many heartbreaks. I will never forget Peter, a brilliant boy from a wealthy family who hated his father because all he cared about was business, success, houses, cars, pleasure. Peter knew there was more to life than that, but he was no more willing to let go of his drugs and immorality than his father was of his materialism. Claiming at first to be an atheist, Peter had finally become convinced by the over-whelming evidence that God exists and that Jesus Christ is the Savior. Still, he always drew back when it came to making a real commitment. I reasoned with Peter day and night, trying to persuade him to receive Christ.

One evening I pleaded with him to delay no longer. "Peter, all of your intellectual arguments are only an excuse," I said. "Your problem isn't intellectual, but moral. You know the truth, and you must make your decision whether to live by it or not. I can't decide for you. Right now, without Christ, your life has no purpose or meaning. You have to de-cide whether to go to school or not, whether to accept a certain job, whether to take drugs, whether to love or to hate . . . and you must also decide to accept or to reject Christ. The choice is Christ or Satan, eternal life or eternal death. It's a decision you can't escape. There's no neutral ground. But you must decide."

The next day Peter put a gun to his head and committed suicide. That news was almost more than I could bear. Had he killed himself because of what I had said? Was my ap-proach wrong? Should I stop working with these young ad-dicts? How could I continue, knowing that this might happen again? I became so discouraged that I couldn't preach any more for several days. I was in agony, haunted day and night by the reminder of Peter's suicide and the possibility that in some way I had precipitated it. Gradually, however, after much prayer, the Lord showed me that I had been offering Peter life, not death. Everyone who rejected Christ was choosing death, even without putting a gun to their heads. Many were destroying themselves with drugs, alcohol, and sexual perversions. But many were choosing new life in Christ. It would help no one for me to remain silent or to give a false impression that the decision wasn't urgent.

My heart continued to ache at the memory of Peter. I saw his haunted expression reflected in the faces of so many others. One could sense the power of evil spirits in their lives. I was sure that demons, like those that had haunted our house and dominated my own life, had influenced Peter to destroy himself. He had placed himself in their power when he had rejected Christ. The evidence of demonic power operating through drugs and Eastern mysticism confronted me daily.

Late one night I stood with two friends just outside that basement we used for meetings. It was empty that night; there was no one sleeping there. We were trying to reason with a young addict named Raymond, who had attempted suicide twice that evening and seemed to be completely out of control. Three weeks before, I had earnestly urged him to give up drugs and to receive Christ. He had mocked me then. And now as the four of us talked, Raymond suddenly pulled me inside the cellar and locked the door behind us almost before I knew what had happened. He was much larger and stronger than I and physically I was powerless to stop him. Once inside, with the door bolted, he began strangling me. As he squeezed my throat with all his frenzied strength, I could feel nothing. Confused by this miracle, he retreated for a moment. I reached out to unbolt the door, and Raymond sprang upon me like a tiger.

"I'm Satan!" he screamed wildly. "Satan is in me!" He threw me against the door and began searching around for a weapon. Picking up a large, heavy bottle filled with syrup for making fruit drinks, he advanced toward me, shouting, "I am Satan! Don't move or I'll smash this bottle into your face!" He raised the bottle behind his head with his arm cocked to throw it.

There was no doubt in my mind that Raymond was possessed by demons that had entered him on his drug trips, just as I, through meditation, had been possessed by evil spirits that had given me the superhuman strength to swing those heavy weights like a club at my aunt's head. The muscular force Raymond now exhibited was awesome. But I knew that the power these evil beings had once held over me had been broken the moment Christ had come into my heart.

"If you're Satan," I replied firmly, "then I'm not going to obey you because I belong to Christ!" I took a step toward him.

Instantly he threw that bottle with all his might. I saw it flashing straight for me and cried out to Jesus. There was not even time to duck. One moment the bottle was about to smash into my face, and the next it had slammed into the door behind me. I felt the wind, and saw it swerve around me as though it had been deflected by an invisible shield.

"Raymond, Jesus loves you and wants to help you," I said, advancing slowly toward him. "Jesus is victor. I'm claiming deliverance for you in the name of the Lord Jesus Christ!"

The demons that were in him couldn't bear to hear the name of Jesus. Raymond put his hands over his ears and began running around the room screaming, "No! No!" Now I was able to remove the bolt and let in my two friends. Just as they entered, Raymond picked up a chair and raised it over his head to smash my skull.

"In the name of Jesus, drop that chair!" I commanded.

It fell to the floor behind him. He was completely wild now. He picked up a heavy portable stove and was aiming that at my head when I said again, "In the name of Jesus, put that down!" The stove fell from his hands.

We began to pray aloud, asking God to bind the spirits

that had possessed Raymond and to cast them out. He ran off into a corner and cowered there like an animal, making strange noises. We continued to pray loudly in the name of Jesus Christ the Lord. Suddenly Raymond cried, "A dark thing has gone out of me! But there's another one inside!" He fell to his knees and began to pray too.

We continued to claim the victory in the name of the Lord Jesus Christ. At last Raymond exclaimed, "It's gone out! It's gone out!" He began to weep like a child. "Please forgive me, Lord," he cried, "for the drugs I've taken and for the homosexual life I've lived!" Apparently he had been earning the money for drugs through homosexual acts. By God's grace Raymond became a new person.

Our methods shocked the Christians in Zurich. "The Evangelicals say the ground here is too hard," Heinz reminded us one day with a twinkle in his eye. "The free churches say you can't win these hippies and addicts and homosexuals and prostitutes to Christ. And the state church says it isn't necessary—if they were baptized as infants and confirmed it will all be okay in the end. Hah!" He exploded with a short laugh. "But God has told us to get out into the streets and win them to Christ. They say it can't be done. Nobody but the Salvation Army does that here. We'll see what God can do."

We were daily seeing fresh proof that "with God all things are possible." We preached to crowds that sometimes swelled to hundreds in front of the train station where four streets converged. It was quite a sight at these meetings to see immovable Swiss coming forward at the invitation to receive Christ. We knew that it wasn't our zeal or talents or determination but the Holy Spirit at work. It seemed that we were just observers watching a revolution gather momentum. One hard-core hippie who had been transformed by Christ and set free from drugs showed his gratitude by giving us his old VW. It made so much noise that we called it "Thunderbird," but it was a great help in the work.

When one of the leaders among the hippie addicts received Christ and was baptized in the lake, it was the talk of Zurich. As the news spread, young people came to us from various churches offering their help. One young woman, challenged by the call to discipleship, gave us her entire savings account, and we used it to purchase a used VW minibus. Some young people came from their churches out of curiosity to see what was happening—and with disastrous results for more than one. Those whose Christianity was not real and personal were often converted by the hippies to their way of life: drugs and mysticism and sexual promiscuity and perversions. How clearly we could see the truth of what Paul had said: "Put on the whole armour of God . . . for we wrestle not against flesh and blood, but against principalities, against powers, against the rulers of the darkness of this world."

We found ourselves in this battle day and night, and we saw many seemingly hopeless cases, who were truly bound by the powers of darkness, set free and transformed by Christ. None who opened their hearts to him were left in bondage to the habits and perversions that had for years dominated their lives. Theological arguments between liberals and evangelicals were meaningless. We saw the daily demonstration in real life that Jesus Christ is indeed the *only way*. Nothing else could bring the complete deliverance that was needed.

When we had burned the idols that memorable day, I was just beginning to understand that Christ had died not only so that I could be forgiven but also to do away with the old Rabi and to give me a new life. Slowly that understanding and the experience of it had grown. In Christ I had died to all I had once been. Through his resurrection he had come to live in me. That was the secret of my new life, and I was seeing it work now in many who were otherwise without hope.

Gradually I had begun to understand that new life out of death—a whole new creation through Christ's death and resurrection—was the theme of the Bible from Genesis to Revelation, the great plan toward which God had been working ever since the fall of Adam and Eve. Christ had not died just to restore Eden's lost Paradise. The human race would only fall again. But Christ had risen from the dead in order to live in us, making a new race of twice-born men whose hearts had become his throne, bringing his kingdom within us. For months I had been meditating on Galatians 2:20: "I am crucified with Christ: nevertheless I live; yet not I, but Christ liveth in me." How true I had found that to be!

The writings of men like Andrew Murray, A. W. Tozer, and Oswald J. Smith were a great help in furthering this understanding. Through their books I saw more clearly than ever the difference between the withdrawal from the world attempted by Buddhist monks and Hindu Yogis and the crucified life and resurrection power available for the believer through Christ. The suppression of physical desires my father had practiced was not the right path. But there was a way of victory over sin in Jesus Christ. I found it so well expressed in Tozer's writings.

> There have been those who have thought that to get themselves out of the way it was necessary to withdraw from society; so they denied all natural human relationships [in their] struggle to mortify their flesh. . . . It is not scriptural to believe that the old Adam nature can be conquered in that manner. . . . It yields to nothing less than the cross.
>
> . . . we want to be saved but we insist that Christ do all the dying. . . . We remain king within the little kingdom of Mansoul and wear our tinsel crown with all the pride of a Caesar. . . .
>
> If we will not die, then . . . our uncrucified flesh will rob us of purity of heart, Christlikeness of character, spiritual insight, fruitfulness.*

The more I experienced of Christ's life in me, the more clearly I could see the mistake that both my father and I

* A. W. Tozer, *The Root of the Righteous* (Harrisburg, Pa.: Christian Publications, Inc., 1955), pp. 65–66.

had made. The self-denial practiced in Eastern mysticism of all kinds was based upon the fallacious belief that man's only problem was wrong thinking and that he need only "realize" that he was God. But if I really was Brahman, then I must have known it in the beginning. What good would it do to "realize" once more what I had already known and forgotten? I would surely forget it again. This was no solution but a lie of Satan calculated to blind men to the fact that their sins have separated them from God. One can't solve a problem simply by denying it. Christ's death for our sins provided a real solution: the forgiveness we need in order to be reconciled to God. And his resurrection gave us a new life that would never end.

If we were willing to die in Christ, accepting his death for us, then we could really live—and only then. How thankful I was that in Christ I had died to all my selfish ambitions. No longer were my prayers requests for God to bless my plans, but a means of learning and submitting to his will.

Believing God's Word, I vowed never to allow defeat in my Christian life. I could see so clearly that Christ had died on the cross to give me victory. Through one verse in particular the Lord had impressed me with this fact: "In all these things we are more than conquerors through him who loved us." I believed it with all my heart.

NINETEEN

New Life

The theological training I received at London Bible College was invaluable. I could hardly train others without being trained myself. And it was a great inspiration to be praying and studying with young people from twenty-five countries who had dedicated their lives to serve Christ. Each weekend I was kept busy in evangelism on one of the school's traveling teams. Tuition with board and room was about 500 pounds a year. Periodically I would get a report from the office saying that funds had been paid into my account; and that continued as long as I was in school. I never learned who my secret donors were.

Each vacation—Christmas, Easter, and summer—I went back to Zurich to help in the work there. The basement of that home for the elderly was turned over to our team in the spring of 1971. Christians in Zurich, mostly the young people themselves whom we were training, donated materials, time, and money to renovate and decorate that large room to turn it into a Christian coffeehouse. We wanted to make it as attractive as we could so that more young people would come there to hear about Christ. By then about 150 believers were attending discipleship classes we were conducting, and some were helping with the work. Everyone thought we ought to have a name for the coffeehouse. The one that got the most votes was "New Life." There was no better description of what had happened to me, or of the transformations we were seeing in so many addicts, prostitutes, homosexuals, and criminals of various kinds. Many others who thought they were Christians because they had been raised in a church and obeyed the laws were meeting Christ personally, and they too were being transformed. We took that name for our work—New Life Fellowship—and this is how we are known today throughout Europe. No longer directly affiliated with Operation Mobilization, we still work closely together.

Out of prayer and experience we adopted certain principles. One of the first was that we would never solicit donations, never take an offering in our meetings, and never tell anyone of our needs. Our trust would be in God and not in men. If we received help from anyone, we wanted it to be because they had responded to him and not to some appeal from us. Another principle was to be motivated only by Christ's love. In love God had given his Son, and because he loved us Christ had died for our sins. We prayed that God would help us to preach Christ and to serve him out of love, not because we hoped for a reward in heaven. Second Timothy 2:2 expressed our third principle: "The things that thou hast heard of me among many witnesses, the same commit thou to faithful men, who shall be able to teach others also." We understood that our primary task was to make disciples who in turn could win others and train them too.

From the very beginning we realized that one basic need was solid Bible teaching and definite training in Christian living. Converts needed to know what they believed and why. It was one thing to begin the Christian life with great enthusiasm, but it was something else to grow daily stronger in the faith and to win others to Christ. The newfound joy might last for days or even weeks, but when the going got tough and doubts came and friends tried to entice them back to the old ways, the temptation to have some more free sex or another drug high could suddenly become overwhelming. It takes much more than enthusiasm to carry one through the real tests and battles of life. We emphasized that Christ had not come just to bring men to heaven but to change the way men live upon earth here and now; that he expected his disciples to *obey* him, not just to believe on him. We preached what Christ said: "And whosoever doth not bear his cross, and come after me, cannot be my disciple." And we made that message crystal clear.

Heinz and Annalies, who had married shortly after coming to Zurich, used their small three-room apartment for "spaghetti evangelism," inviting young people in from the streets for dinner and discussion. Eventually the ministry spread to a huge old house of four floors and fourteen rooms. That became home for the team and for hundreds of hippies who stopped there for a night or two or three and heard of Christ. Many abandoned their plans to follow the drug trail into India and went back to apologize to parents they had hated but now loved with Christ's love. But that old house on Mohrlistrasse, where our first eight-month discipleship school began in 1973, was soon too small. In 1974, in what had once been a large retirement home, we began the first class of a three-year Bible School that heavily emphasizes practical training. We hand-picked the students after observing them closely on summer missions. Consequently nearly all went into full-time Christian service. About six months of the third year were spent in practical evangelistic work in one of the several cities in Europe where we had teams based. Each team trusted the Lord for its own needs and its ties with New Life Fellowship were spiritual, not organizational. In 1975 we moved into larger quarters in the village of Walzenhausen overlooking Lake Constance in northeastern Switzerland. Parts of Germany and Austria as well as Switzerland could be seen in the inspiring panorama below us.

The entire team shared my concern to counteract the influence of Eastern mysticism that is now spreading so rapidly in the West. Since becoming a Christian I had seen the average Western mind take on a thoroughly Eastern orientation. The influence of such drug gurus as Timothy Leary, Alan Watts, and Allen Ginsberg is so Hinduistic that it blends with and complements the teachings of Hindu gurus like Muktananda, Maharaj Ji, and Maharishi Mahesh Yogi. This new consciousness born from a blend of drugs and mysticism has largely taken over the thinking on the university campus, the conversation at clubs and cocktail parties, the movie industry, and television. When I visited Maharishi's world headquarters not far from Walzenhausen shortly after he had appeared on the "Merv Griffin Show," I was told that about one million Americans had turned on to TM as a result of that one program. TM is sugarcoated Hinduism deceptively described in scientific terms with denials of its religious nature in order to deceive the Westerner.

Feeling a responsibility to expose such deliberate and clever lies, I began to speak out more bluntly in public to warn those who were being drawn into Yoga, meditation and other forms of Eastern mysticism of the satanic trap they were falling into. Invitations began to come for me to speak at universities on comparative religions or to contrast Hinduism with Christianity. After all, I had seen it from both sides. Soon I was receiving invitations to speak in many countries. It was no longer possible to confine myself to Europe.

While in Israel in the midst of a tour through many countries near the end of 1972, I felt led through prayer to fly home to Trinidad for my first visit there since I had left for London. Although the flights were all sold out and had waiting lists due to the heavy holiday traffic, by God's grace I got a seat from Tel Aviv to London and another from there to Port of Spain without any delays. A friend happened to be at the airport when I landed and gave me a ride right to the old house. It seemed a miracle when I climbed the stairs and walked into the sitting room at about fifteen minutes before midnight. It was Christmas Eve.

"Rabi! This is a gift from God!" exclaimed Ma. "I've been asking him please to send you here for Christmas!" What a reunion we had after six years!

Ma was growing older and seemed much feebler than when I had left, but she was still praising God and still a testimony for Christ. We had some good times praying and discussing the Word of God together, reminiscing over those early days when we had just become Christians. After all those years we still could not get over the change Christ had made in our family and in our individual lives. It was a great joy to see old friends, Christians and Hindus alike, and I had the privilege of preaching the gospel all over Trinidad.

Soon after my return to Europe word came that Ma was seriously ill. She lingered for several weeks, seemed momentarily to recover, then word came that she had gone to be with the Lord. At the funeral there was none of the loud wailing that had accompanied the deaths of Nana and my father and that always mark the passing of a Hindu. We knew that her soul and spirit were with Christ in a new dimension of life in heaven, not reincarnated into some other body to begin another round of pain and sorrow here on earth. I would see Ma again one day at Christ's return, and that could be at any time—the signs all point toward that. In the meanwhile, I was grateful to God for giving me that last visit with Ma before he took her from us. The memory of her Christlike life and the many hours she spent on her knees in prayer would remain a challenge and inspiration to me to continue to serve Christ with my whole heart, just as she had once again urged me to do during our last days together.

In the winter of 1975 one of my dreams came true at last. Five of our staff and eighteen students went on our first training mission into the East. One of our objectives is to train young people to go to countries like Pakistan and India to carry the message of Christ. We are offering scholarships to select students who will witness for Christ while attending universities in India, Bangladesh, Pakistan, Afghanistan, Nepal. One of my objectives on this trip was to make contacts for this program.

In Yugoslavia two of our three VW minibuses were

stopped and the passengers arrested for distributing Christian literature. After some hours they were released and we continued East. On our way through Turkey I had the joy of preaching for the first time in a Muslim country and saw some Muslims receive Christ. In Istanbul it was a great encouragement to stay in the home of a young couple who had become Christians in Zurich three years before, and to see that they were serving their Lord and growing in the faith. The young man belonged to one of Turkey's wealthiest families. He had been living like a playboy with a French girl friend in Switzerland, both of them on drugs, when I had shared the gospel with them at our center in Zurich just before leaving to hold a crusade in Munich during the 1972 Olympic Games. They had both prayed the sinner's prayer and received Christ. His father had threatened to disinherit him—and he had replied that Christ was worth more than the whole world. These two had been married and were now winning others to the Lord in Turkey.

In Pakistan we saw a good response to the gospel. My interpreters in the meetings there were two young Swiss. Several years before, they had followed the drug trail into India, becoming deeply involved in drugs and Eastern mysticism. Miraculously God had reached them while they were living in Pakistan, where they had both received Christ. Returning to Switzerland, they had joined our discipleship school, and on that trip they were able to interpret for me into Urdu as I preached throughout Pakistan.

Lack of time had forced the rest of the team to turn back toward Switzerland. I had continued on toward India, intending to make further contacts and to do some preaching before visiting my mother near Bombay, where she was living in her guru's temple. I had had no problem entering Pakistan, but as I tried to leave I was arrested, as already described. Certain that they had caught a big fish in their net—it's not every day one comes across a spy—the border officials sent word to headquarters in Lahore. The top man himself would want to question me more closely before I was disposed of in the summary fashion deserved by an Indian espionage agent.

Except for the armed guard just outside my door, I was left alone while we all awaited the arrival of the Chief. They had told me that he was a very holy man, one who had made three pilgrimages to Mecca. How that qualified him to be the top police officer in Lahore I didn't know, but it didn't help my position. A devout Muslim would hardly be more lenient on a Christian than on a Hindu, yet my only chance seemed to be to convince the Chief that I was a Christian. Furthermore, I was committed to share Christ with every person I could.

During those three hours waiting under guard alone in that small room, a whole kaleidescope of memories passed before me. I had no regrets at having come to Pakistan. If, through my being there, only one person had received forgiveness of sins and eternal life through Christ, then it had been more than worth it. And many had received Christ. Perhaps I would not be able to convince the Chief that I was not a spy—or a Hindu. The other officers were all convinced that I was lying. How they hated Hindus! To them my death would be a partial revenge for the thousands of fellow Muslims murdered by Hindus. And believing that I was an Indian spy would make that revenge all the sweeter.

There is no better time to test one's faith than in the face of possible death, and now I was more confident than ever that Christ loved me and that physical death could only usher my soul and spirit into his presence where Ma had already preceded me. My heart was full of joy as I thought of all that Christ had done in my life and of the many others whom I had seen transformed through faith in him. I was in God's hands, desiring only his will and whatever would be to his glory, remembering Paul's desire expressed from prison, that "Christ shall be magnified in my body, whether it be by life or by death." I thought of Tozer's writings—one of his books was in my briefcase—and of Galatians 2:20, on which I had meditated for so many years. "I am crucified with Christ: nevertheless I live; yet not I, but Christ liveth in me." I had already died in him, so death could not touch me. I had no fear of what these men might do.

"Why are you spying here in our country?" was the only greeting the Chief gave me when at last he arrived.

"But I'm not a spy," I protested. "I wouldn't do that."

He seemed amused. "You wouldn't? Why not?"

"Because I'm a Christian."

"*You* a Christian? Isn't this your passport?" he asked, pointing to it lying on the desk in front of him. "Maharaj is not a Christian name, not by any means." The look in his eyes said that it was an insult to his intelligence to imagine that he would believe such a fantastic lie.

"Yes, my name *is* Maharaj, but I *am* a Christian," I insisted.

"Prove it." Now he was smiling as though enjoying a secret joke.

That was a shock. I had never thought of that before. How could I ever prove what I believed in my heart? There was no one here who knew me, no witnesses to testify of my life. . . .

"Are you a Muslim?" I asked respectfully.

"Yes, I am."

"Can you *prove* that you're a Muslim?" Surely he would see how utterly unreasonable he was being.

"Why should I have to?" he shot back. "I'm not the spy!"

"But *I'm* not a spy either!"

"Then prove that you're a Christian!" Again that smile.

"Well," I said, opening my briefcase, "here's my Bible. Would a Hindu carry a Bible?"

He laughed. "A clever spy would!"

I began turning the pages under his nose. "But look, sir, see how it's all underlined, page after page, the verses that have some special meaning for me. . . ."

"Any spy could do that."

I reached into my briefcase again. "Here are other Christian books . . . and look at these letters from people I've led to Christ, see what they say."

He waved my latest "evidence" away without giving it a glance. "Do you think I'm stupid? Easily faked, all of it."

I was stunned. There was no way to *prove* I was a Christian. Then I thought of something else. "I have one other piece of evidence," I said, reaching into my briefcase for the last time. "If this doesn't convince you. . . . It's a manuscript, the story of my life." I laid it on the desk in front of him. "It tells everything: my life as a Hindu and how I became a follower of Jesus the Messiah. No spy would think of faking something like that . . . not that many pages!"

Giving me a skeptical look, he opened the manuscript and began to read. This was my last hope. As he turned page after page, I alternately prayed and watched his expression. At chapter fourteen, "Death of a Guru"—nothing beyond that had been written at that time—he began to read more slowly, apparently absorbed in the story of how I had given my heart to Christ. Near the end, as he read about the smashing and burning of the idols, he grunted approvingly and nodded his head. The Koran denounces idolatry, and Muslims had destroyed many Hindu idols and temples in their conquest of India centuries before. Slowly and carefully he read that chapter again. Then he handed the manuscript back to me.

"I'm convinced you're a Christian," he said, but the expression on his face had not softened. "But what were you doing in our country?"

How could I answer that? Had I jumped from the frying pan into the fire? I had heard of Christians being killed recently in Pakistan for telling Muslims about Christ. Others had been given long prison terms. Asking God for wisdom, I chose my words carefully.

"You have a great country," I said sincerely, "but you also have many problems. I came with a team of twenty-two others from Switzerland. We visited hospitals, orphanages, leprosariums, trying to help in any way we could, physically and spiritually. We love your people and your land. Although our help is small, we have done what we could."

He had been watching me closely. Now he leaned back in his chair and let out a long breath. The expression on his face relaxed for the first time. He opened my passport, reached wearily for a rubber stamp, and pressed it firmly onto the page that bore the record of my entry into his country. Handing the passport to me he said, "You can go!"

Grateful to God, I walked past the armed guard and out of that room, a free man. The officers who had interrogated me earlier and who were waiting outside expressed their amazement to me. They could not believe that I was being allowed to leave.

Crossing the hundred yards of no-man's-land to the Indian border station, I thanked the Lord for his grace and prayed that the high Muslim official would be won to Christ by the story he had read. He had been convinced of its truthfulness, and the expression on his face as he read had told me that he had been deeply moved by my conversion to Christ.

My problems, however, were not over yet. I was promptly taken into an inner office for questioning by Indian officials. They seemed to think I was a Pakistani spy.

"You must be a Pakistani," the official in charge insisted. "No Indian would be in Pakistan. What were you doing there?"

"I'm a follower of Christ, and I was doing Christian work there."

"You, a Brahmin, a Christian? Untouchables become Christians, but not *Brahmins*. I don't believe you."

"Well, I can tell you how it happened." I launched into my story, trying to make it brief, and he listened with growing interest. When I had finished he shook his head slowly in amazement, opened my passport, pressed the entry stamp on a blank page, and scribbled his signature. "Have a good trip," he said pleasantly.

It is impossible to describe India to those who have not seen it for themselves. The misery, poverty, disease, and superstition are staggering. If the villages present a shocking picture, one is completely overwhelmed by the horror of existence for the countless millions that crowd India's cities. My host in Calcutta told me that more than a million eke out a pitiful existence in the streets of that city without even a mud hut to call home. They die where they were born—in a gutter or alley or on a filthy sidewalk in the hot sun—having known nothing but the misery of disease and poverty, and the hopelessness of trying to appease or appeal to deities that show not the slightest love or concern and only demand more fear. To live and die in such wretched, abject misery, and yet to be told that you are God and only need to "realize" it—who could devise a more macabre joke than that? And to be told that the running sores on your body, the gnawing hunger in your stomach, and the deeper emptiness in your soul are only maya, an illusion . . . could there be a more diabolical deception?

My heart ached as I viewed India's suffering masses. I marveled that Westerners were looking to India for spiritual insight. From experience I knew that Hinduism, with its fatalistic belief in karma, reincarnation, and false gods, was the root of India's problems. What blindness for Westerners to turn to Eastern mysticism for enlightenment! It held nothing but darkness, and India's plight bore eloquent testimony as to how deep that darkness really was. Such enormous deception could only be put across by the same devilishly clever source that convinces millions to destroy themselves for the sake of a phony paradise they experience when stoned on drugs.

It was a happy but also a strange and somewhat tense experience to see my mother once again, the third time in twenty-one years. Shortly after I left Trinidad for England, she had suddenly quit the temple in Port of Spain, dropping that prestigious position where she had seemingly been so happy. With money her wealthy friends had raised for furniture, books, and equipment, she had started a school for girls.

Everyone had confidence that with her in charge it would be a first-class institution of learning. Although it was supposed to be nonsectarian, she had placed a heavy emphasis upon Yoga in the curriculum, teaching that course to the students herself. Then abruptly one weekend, without any notice or warning, she had simply packed her bags and vanished. Monday morning when the girls returned to school they found it locked, without even a note of explanation pinned to the door. Aunt Revati later had learned that my mother had been ordered to the New York temple of her guru, Baba Muktananda. After nearly a year spent there helping to recruit disciples for Muktananda from among wealthy Americans, she had returned to his main temple in India with a group of new converts and had been there ever since in a position of great responsibility.

There were about a hundred young Westerners in Muktananda's temple near Bombay when I arrived, far less than usual, because most of them were away for a few days during the holidays. This popular guru's complex of high-rise buildings stands like an oasis of prosperity and affluence in the midst of the most miserable poverty on every side.

To be living once again in a Hindu temple—what memories came back to me, and how clearly I sensed the darkness and oppression of evil spirits! I was thankful, however, for the opportunity to speak earnestly with many of the Westerners who were living and studying there. "Look at the misery all around you," I would say compassionately. "With her vast natural resources and manpower, India should be one of the wealthiest countries in the world—but she has been ruined by her religious philosophy. It's heartbreaking! Why, in spite of all this, are you accepting Hinduism?"

"We're sick of Western materialism," they would reply.

"Today India is trying desperately to get Western technology—and materialism," I would remind them, "hoping to save her starving millions. Not just Westerners, but lots of wealthy Hindus, too, are materialistic. Hinduism won't deliver you from that, but Christ can. Look at what Muktananda has built with the money he has gotten in the West. How much of it has he used to help the starving, miserable people in the little shacks surrounding this wealthy property? Christ is the only hope for you, or me . . . or India. And the materialism you have rejected is not Christianity."

My mother looked thin and not too well. The regime was rigorous, beginning at 3:30 A.M. each day with several hours of yoga and meditation. Mother and I had some good visits, but I found it impossible to say a word about Christ to her, knowing that to do so would shatter the fragile relationship we were trying to reestablish. But I prayed daily that the Lord would allow me to have a few days with her away from the overpowering presence of demons in that temple.

To my joy, after I had been with her for about four days, my mother agreed to come into Bombay with me. Some friends of mine had offered their house for us to stay in while they were away. It seemed like a dream. Mother was cooking the meals, the tension was gradually easing, we were friends once again, living in a home together once more after so many long years. I tried to do nothing that would disturb the tranquillity of our new relationship, enjoying each moment; pushing from my mind every reminder of how brief it would have to be. We went window shopping and sightseeing and took walks together, and we grew to know and understand one another again after such a long separation, gently and with increasing confidence opening our hearts to each other like two strangers.

Then one unforgettable afternoon the fragile new relationship we were trying to build together suddenly shattered into a thousand irretrievable pieces. I had carefully refrained from saying a word that would disturb her. Not a hint of the fact that I was a Christian had passed my lips, only a few careful questions about the obvious misery we saw everywhere. Could *that* be the result of thousands of years of karma and upward evolution toward God through reincarnation that she talked about constantly? She never tried to answer that question, just went on and on enthusiastically—trying a bit too hard to seem happy, I thought—about yoga and meditation and her responsibilities in the temple and much praise for her guru, Muktananda, whom she spoke of again and again as though he were God. That afternoon, however, it finally became too much for me to bear in silence any longer. It was false for me to keep quiet as though I agreed with her.

"Please, Mommy, your guru isn't God," I said suddenly, surprising even myself. "No man has the right to call himself that."

"Well, your Jesus said that *he* was God," she responded quickly, as though she had been waiting and hoping I would make such a comment. "Baba is only saying what Jesus said about himself too."

I looked at her with sorrow. "But Mommy," I said earnestly, "when Jesus says he's God, *he really is God,* and the Bible does show it to be true—but your guru is only a man."

She had been stirring some food on the stove. Now she whirled around to face me. "You've insulted my guru and my religion, and I'm not going to bear it any longer! If this is why you came—just to convert me to Christianity—then don't bother ever coming back!" She hurried from the room, leaving me almost too shocked to move. In a moment I heard her moving around above in the bedroom she had been using; then her footsteps slowly descended the stairs. I met her in the living room.

"I'm leaving," she said abruptly.

"Mommy, you can't do that," I protested, taking the little suitcase from her hand and putting it on the floor. "Please don't go!"

She picked up her suitcase and resolutely went out the front door. I watched through the window, feeling helpless and shattered, as she said good-bye to some people living on the same property that she had become acquainted with. Then she disappeared down the street carrying her small bag.

Running into my room, I fell across the bed, feeling utterly desolate, scarcely able to pray. *Lord*, I pleaded, *after all these years, is this all I can say to my mother about you? If she doesn't come back now, I may never see her again! Please bring her back!* I continued to pray, but I was in such agony of soul that I fell asleep in my sorrow.

When I awakened it had grown dark. Someone was moving around in the bedroom my mother had been using. Sitting up, I listened. Could it be? Then everything became quiet; I heard nothing but the sound of my own breathing. I waited as long as I could stand the suspense, then went cautiously up to her room. She was lying on the bed.

"May I bring you something for supper?" I asked.

She mumbled a faint "No" and turned her face away. I went downstairs and fixed myself something to eat. All remained quiet upstairs. Several hours later I asked her if I could bring her something to drink, but the response was the same. I prayed a good part of that night for her. The next day she again refused my hesitant offers of food or drink and remained secluded in her room. In the evening a friend from Operation Mobilization joined me and we prayed for hours under my mother's room.

The next morning she came into the kitchen and fixed breakfast as though nothing had happened. Conversing together, we carefully avoided any mention of that unhappy incident and stayed away from subjects that might lead to a recurrence. It was the day before Christmas, the first one we would spend together in twenty-one years. I had some business to take care of at a Christian bookstore in Bombay, my last chance before it closed for the holidays. With my mother's permission I went there in the late afternoon. After our discussion, as the manager and I walked from his office to the front door, I noticed a book with an interesting title —*Theology: Hindu and Christian*—and bought a copy for myself. It would have helpful information for the many talks I made on that subject.

When I returned to the house, Mother was already preparing our supper. I stopped in the kitchen, and we were talking together when my friend from Operation Mobilization came in.

"Here's something I want to give you, Rabi," he said, handing a book to me. "I know you're interested in this subject."

Taking the book from him I began to laugh. "Thank you," I said sincerely, "but I just bought the same book an hour ago. What a coincidence!" I opened the bag I had laid on the table and pulled out the other copy, then laid them beside each other. "Now what am I going to do with two books of the same title?" I asked jokingly.

My mother had been watching and listening. She leaned over and seemed to study the title: *Theology: Hindu and Christian.* Suddenly she said, "You could give one to me."

I almost gasped in surprise. It was hard to keep from shouting, Praise the Lord! Never could I have dared to offer such a book to her. And even now she didn't hold out her hand. I left them on the table. As soon as supper was finished she picked up one copy and went upstairs to her room, where I was sure she began to read it. Now I saw the opportunity to do something I had been waiting years for.

Calling the manager of the bookstore at his home, I asked if he would do a special favor for me. "I know the store is closed for the holidays," I said, "but could I somehow purchase a copy of the *Living Bible?*"

He was very willing to help me, especially when I confided in him that it was for my mother to take back to her temple.

Mother and I had a quiet and amiable Christmas together. In the afternoon we both had to leave Bombay, she to go back to her guru's temple and I to fly to Switzerland where I would be delivering a paper at a Youth Congress on World Missions concerning the challenge presented by the increasing influence of Eastern mysticism in the West. As we parted, I handed her the Bible wrapped in bright Christmas paper.

"Make me a promise," I said with a smile, "that you won't open this until you get back to the temple."

"I promise," she said happily, "but I think I already know what it is." She was feeling its weight, and I was sure she thought it was a box of chocolates.

"No, you don't!" I said with a laugh. "It will be a real surprise, but I know you'll like it."

A few weeks later a letter from Mother caught up with me in the United States. In part it said, "Thank you so much for the Bible, Rabi. I keep it under my pillow and read it every day. I would like to leave the temple and come to live with you."

Epilogue

Rabi is very much on the go, preaching in Germany, France, Austria, South America, Canada . . . not an easy person to reach by long-distance phone. But this time I caught him at his office in Switzerland. He had encouraged me to come for a visit, assuring me we could spend some time together.

As my plane landed in Zurich and taxied to the terminal, my thoughts went back three years to that day in Paris when Rabi and I had first met. He had told me part of his remarkable story then, and I suggested that it ought to be shared with the world—never dreaming that he would take my advice, much less that our paths would cross again a year later in Lausanne at the World Congress on Evangelization. We had been close friends ever since, but this would be my first visit to the New Life Fellowship headquarters in Walzenhausen.

An early partial draft of his book had probably saved Rabi's life at the Pakistan-India border. Now the manuscript was finished and I would have the opportunity of going over it with him before he submitted it to the publisher. Knowing the story so well, I was eager to ask Rabi what had happened in the intervening years to some of the main characters.

When I came through passport control with my suitcase, a young woman of about twenty-five walked up to me. "You must be Mr. Hunt," she said. With my height, bald head, and beard I wasn't too difficult to identify.

"Yes, I am." It was not yet 6 A.M., and I had asked Rabi not to have anyone meet me; it was too much of an imposition, and anyway I was an old hand at getting around in Europe.

"I'm Renate. Rabi mentioned that you were coming, and I offered to drive you to the train station. Bus service isn't very good this early."

"That's awfully kind of you . . . I really hadn't expected it."

Inside her sports coupe on the way to the Bahnhof, I asked my standard question: "When did you become a Christian?"

That query uncovered one of the many fascinating stories that Rabi had not told me. There were simply too many.

"It happened three years ago," said Renate. "My sister, Inge, a hopeless drug addict, was in the hospital dying of an incurable disease that was destroying her blood. The doctors gave her only a few more hours. Mother had already made funeral arrangements. Then she heard of Rabi and the work he was doing with drug addicts."

I was hanging on every word now. Here was a story that Rabi ought to have put in the book—but one can't include everything. Nor was Renate telling all. I learned later that her own life had been a hopeless tangle of alcoholism and free sex.

"Rabi and his cousin Ananda came to the hospital, shared the gospel with my sister, and prayed for her. She opened her heart to Christ before they left. To the amazement of the doctors, Inge was healed. I, too, became a Christian—in the coffeehouse the following evening. And my mother also received Christ."

So Ananda was in Europe, too, and still living for Christ. That was good to know.

"Amar is here, too," Renate added, "studying German like Ananda and singing at some of Rabi's meetings. He's living with the Heddingers right here in Zurich."

The Heddingers. There were so many names, all part of the story. I thumbed through the files in my memory. Yes, they had taken Rabi in when he first came to Zurich, treated him like a son. So the relationship had lasted through the years. And now they had taken in Amar, Aunt Revati's youngest child, who, like Rabi, had also been a very religious Hindu at a young age. Ananda and Amar had followed Rabi to Switzerland. More important, they were still following Christ, still serving him after all these years. That was the sort of information I was interested in.

Snow was beginning to fall lightly just outside Zurich. The two-hour ride by rail through the beautiful Swiss countryside was climaxed by a steep climb up the mountain in a small-gauge cog train to the picturesque village of Walzenhausen. This was real "Sound of Music" country, high above Bregenz, Austria, and with a breathtaking view of Lake Constance far below. In response to my request for directions to New Life Fellowship, the train conductor, who also doubled as stationmaster and ticket vendor, pointed out "*das grosses braunes Haus*" perched on a steep slope about a mile away. He offered to phone. In a few minutes a VW pulled up in front of the tiny station. Rabi jumped out and ran to greet me, hands extended, his face glowing with that irrepressible smile.

The students I met at the discipleship training school in New Life's "*grosses braunes Haus*" impressed me very much. They were almost all recent converts of two, three, four years—but with a surprising maturity that seems to come more quickly to those who let go of everything else to really follow Christ. Classes were held in a large chalet next door to the living quarters and offices. There was even a swimming pool, also used for baptisms, with six inches of fresh snow now on the bottom. And the orderliness and efficiency with which everything was run impressed me almost as much as the dedication and zeal of those involved. These people not only meant business for their Lord but they went about it intelligently and realistically. Rabi had told me that Heinz

206

was a great organizer, but everything seemed to run without any obvious supervision from him. There was no personality cult, no exaltation of the founders that I could detect.

"Rabi's Aunt Revati was here a few weeks ago," one of the students mentioned casually one morning at breakfast. And someone else, a little later, showed me a picture of an attractive and dynamic woman in a sari seated among some of the students, her face aglow with a smile quite like Rabi's. It was hard to visualize her as a religious Hindu fanatically worshiping Kali, the blood-drinking, murderous goddess that had been her favorite. *What a difference Christ has made!* That thought kept running through my mind as Rabi and I went over the story together during the next ten days. Yes, what a difference. I saw it in Rabi, and I heard of the transformation Christ effects as we talked of some of the others involved and I asked him what they were doing now.

"Aunt Revati is winning Hindus to Christ," Rabi told me happily. "She especially loves to spread the gospel in out-of-the-way Indian villages where they speak mainly Hindi. She holds meetings for children and women and has even been invited to speak in some of the temples. Imagine being able to tell about Christ in a Hindu temple!"

I was particularly interested to know what had happened to another of his aunts—Mohanee, his father's sister. "Did she become a Christian?" I asked.

Rabi shook his head sadly. "No. I went to see her a few months ago when I was last in Trinidad. She made no response when I tried to talk to her. She has become just like my father, whom she worshiped. Just stares and says nothing. Has to be cared for like she once cared for him. One would think that the same spirit that possessed him now possesses her."

And Krishna? I learned that he graduated from Yale and is now working on his Ph.D. at Harvard while serving as the assistant pastor of an evangelical church in the Boston area. Uncle Lari is a professor in a university on the East Coast of the United States, and the latest one in the family to become a Christian. It was the writings of C. S. Lewis that convinced his brilliant mind. He surrendered his heart to Christ and is steadily growing in the faith.

Sandra is also in Switzerland, for further nursing experience, and hopes to go to the mission field soon. "Shanti is in London," Rabi told me, "and still serving the Lord. And Brendan Bain, my best friend from Youth for Christ at Queen's Royal College . . . he's a medical doctor now, in Jamaica, with a lovely family, a really fruitful Christian, serving the Lord in many ways."

Sitting in the living room of the home Rabi shares with Annalies, Heinz, and their three young children—and assorted guests and staff members from time to time—I looked across beautiful Lake Constance to Germany and at Austria and Switzerland just below me on this side, and thought how remarkable it was that so many of those who were part of Rabi's story had been scattered to the four winds around the world to tell others about Christ.

"What about Molli?" I asked eagerly. To me she was one of the most interesting characters. What courage God had given this girl! "Where is she now, and what is she doing?"

Rabi smiled. "I just spent a few days with her and her family last June in New York. She married the young man who shared the gospel with my cousin Krishna. They have two lovely children. Molli's an R.N. and her husband is studying medicine. They're preparing for the mission field."

"The whole world is a mission field, brother!" Heinz Strupler told me when I first met him. He was just like Rabi had described—with his own built-in loudspeaker for preaching anywhere, a bundle of energy and zeal, all of it dedicated to Christ. And with a sense of humor that kept his superdedication from becoming a burden. "You can't imagine how unorthodox our methods seemed at first to European Christians," Heinz said. "And what resistance we met to the message of true Christianity and discipleship in the churches. You know how the Swiss and Germans run everything by the clock," he added with a twinkle in his eyes. "I remember once George Verwer—he's one of the founders of Operation Mobilization—was preaching in a large church in West Germany, saying what God wanted him to say and never mind the time. Finally, one of the pastors tried to get him to stop. He was standing in the back of the church waving his watch. George looked at him and said, 'Praise the Lord! That brother in the back wants to give his watch for the needs in Bangladesh!' That ended the watch-waving, and George went on telling of the great need to deny ourselves, take up the cross, and follow Christ."

The other New Life Fellowship staff members whom I met all seemed to have the same passion to get the gospel of Christ to the world. Already over 300 young people they have trained have gone out to spend their lives sharing Christ in many countries. About 85 students are in the discipleship training school now. They hope to expand but not to grow so large that they lose the personal contact with each student that is so important.

Rabi's face still lights up whenever he talks of Ma. Her prayer life especially had a great influence upon him. "She had very few possessions," he told me. "Just a few clothes. The only things she left behind when she died were several large boxes full of letters from friends and her many children and grandchildren around the world . . . and one other thing, her most prized possession. It was a Bible given to her by Deonarine . . . on Mother's Day. She took a lot of comfort from that. It gave her hope that he had become a Christian before he died. Uncle Kumar has it now in London."

When Rabi talks of the future, he keeps coming back to one theme: the need to combat the influence of Eastern mysticism that is sweeping the West. Millions who once believed in Christ's resurrection, at least as a historical fact, now believe instead in reincarnation. The idea that Jesus of Nazareth was just one of many reincarnations of the "Christ spirit" that was supposedly also in Rama, Krishna, Buddha, among others, is becoming increasingly popular, paving the way for the AntiChrist to pose as its latest reincarnation. The personal

God of the Bible is being confused, in many minds, with Nature or Cosmic Forces or Maharishi's Natural Laws, or Paul Tillich's Ground of Being. All are Westernized versions of the Hindu's Brahman.

"I'm praying about opening a Center for Eastern Studies somewhere in Switzerland," said Rabi. "It would be a place where people who have been taken in by TM or Yoga or other forms of Eastern mysticism such as Zen, Eckankar, est—they're almost without number—could come for counseling to get themselves sorted out and meet Christ. And Christians could study there to prepare themselves to share Christ with those who have developed an Eastern way of thinking. There's a whole new breed of people in the West now, especially in the universities, with whom the average Christian no longer communicates, but without realizing it. There are millions of such Westerners, and their number is growing rapidly."

From my guestroom in the school, watching Rabi come down a steep, snow-clogged path for another session of going over the manuscript, it all seems very much like a dream. It's so implausible to see an East Indian walking through a blinding snowstorm with Swiss chalets all around. He sees me looking out of the window now, waves, and smiles. I think of Rabi at sixteen in Trinidad, praying that foolish prayer—for God to let him preach the gospel to a million people—and realize that he has preached to several million now.

Rabi arrives in my room still stamping the snow from his feet. Pulling off his coat, he begins to talk about the future of the school and his own ministry. There is deep satisfaction in his voice, and that perpetual smile reflects an inner peace that nothing seems to disturb. The conversation turns to the proposed Center for Eastern Studies. I tell Rabi how much I agree that it is badly needed and how great it would be if his mother, after all her years in Hinduism, could be part of its staff.

He nods slowly. "That would be so wonderful. My mother is really searching for the Truth, but there's still a spiritual battle going on. She has to get away from her guru. I'm praying very much that she'll open her heart fully to Christ—and soon."

"I'll pray for her, too, brother!" I promise.

I had hoped so much to meet Rabi's mother, hoped that she would be in Switzerland by the time I arrived. But she's still at the temple near Bombay. That's not the way the story should end—but of course it hasn't ended.

Dave Hunt
Walzenhausen, Switzerland
December 1976

Glossary

ahimsa The doctrine of nonviolence toward all life. Since the Hindu believes that insects and animals, through good karma, evolve upward to become humans—and that humans, through bad karma, may become animals or insects again—it would be tantamount to murder and cannibalism to kill and eat any living thing except plants. The Hindu must therefore be a vegetarian.

Ahimsa, however, is not consistent either with the Hindu scriptures or practice. Many Hindus still make animal sacrifices, and throughout history, Hindus have not demonstrated any less propensity to kill an enemy in wars and revolutions than men not professing the doctrine of ahimsa. Hindus have, however, consistently refrained from killing cows.

arti A religious ritual performed by rotating the sacred flame or incense—held on a platter in the right hand—in a clockwise circle around the replica of a god or saint. This can be done by any Hindu in his own prayer room.

ashram From the Hindi word *asrama*, signifying the four "stages" in life of the twice-born (high-caste) Hindu: (1) adolescence as a celibate religious student; (2) married householder who begets children; (3) a time of retreat into the forest for meditation and devotion to religious duties and rituals; and (4) old age, when one is expected to renounce all possessions except loincloth, begging bowl, and water pot, live by begging, and be free from all obligations and observances. The term has come to be applied more to the third "stage" in life, as well as to the hermitage of a sage.

Today it is popularly used for a religious community or retreat in India, usually where one goes to study under a guru, and even some Christian organizations in India now call their retreats "ashrams."

avatar   In its broadest sense, the incarnation of any god into any living form. Every species presumably has its own avatars. In the narrower sense, however, an avatar is a reincarnation of Vishnu. Some Hindus hold that Vishnu has been reincarnated innumerable times, while others teach that he has come as an avatar only nine times: as a fish, a tortoise, a man-lion, a boar, and a child-dwarf, and as Rama, Krishna, Buddha, and Christ.

The exact role that the avatar plays in bringing salvation to man is not clear, but the avatar is generally considered to function as a guru in each reincarnation. Many orthodox Hindus believe that Kalki, the next avatar after Christ, is due to appear on earth in about 425,000 years. However, there are hundreds of gurus today who are considered by their followers to be avatars.

barahi   Meaning "twelve," a religious ceremony held on the twelfth day after the birth of a male Brahmin, at which time the pundits and astrologers make predictions concerning the child's future.

Bhagavad-Gita   The most popular of the Hindu scriptures, part of the Mahabharata, and the most widely read of any Hindu holy book in the East or West. Known as "The Song of the Lord" and often called "the gospel of Hinduism," the Gita is a dialogue between the warrior Arjuna, who shrinks from killing his relatives in the war he faces, and the avatar-god Krishna, who acts as his charioteer and encourages him to do his duty in battle as a good and brave warrior.

Bhagwan   A Hindi word for God or Lord.

bhai   Literally "brother," a term of honor given to one's equal. Rarely would an older religious Hindu use this term in addressing an adolescent and never to a child. Therefore when Gosine began to address Rabi in this way it was an indication that he had transferred to him the honor and esteem with which he had regarded his father.

bhajans   Songs of devotional love used in worship of the gods.

Bliss The state of being achieved when the illusion of existence apart from Brahman, who is pure existence-knowledge-bliss, has been dispelled through meditation and enlightenment and all desires have ceased. Since this state is said to be beyond pain or pleasure, Buddha, who was raised a Hindu, thought of it as "nothingness," which he also called "nirvana."

Brahma Not to be confused with Brahman, who is all gods in One, Brahma, the Creator, is the first god in the Hindu tri murti The others are Vishnu, the Preserver, and Shiva, the Destroyer. Supposedly every 4.32 billion years Shiva destroys everything, Brahma creates all again, and Vishnu is reincarnated once more to reveal the path to Brahman. Often depicted as issuing from Vishnu's navel (which seems to contradict his role as Creator), Brahma is usually shown with four heads and four hands holding sacrificial instruments, prayer beads, and a manuscript.

Brahmacharya Literally "religious living," the name given to the first of four stages in the high-caste Hindu's life. Since this was a time during which sexual abstinence was obligatory, the word also came to be applied to older religious Hindus still living under this vow of celibacy.

Brahman The Ultimate Reality: formless, inexpressible, unknowable, and unknowing; neither personal nor impersonal; both Creator and all that is created. Brahman is all and all is Brahman.

The ultimate truth and salvation for the Hindu is to "realize" that he is himself Brahman, that he and all the universe are one and the same Being. However, Brahman is not just another name for the God of the Bible but a concept foreign and opposed to the Judeo-Christian God. Brahman is everything and yet nothing; it comprises both good and evil, life and death, health and disease, and even the unreality of maya.

Brahmin The highest Hindu caste and closest human form to Brahman through thousands of reincarnations, and therefore the intermediary between Brahman and the other castes. One must be a Brahmin to be a priest. This gives the Brahmins great power over the other castes; however, Brahmins are required to live a much more religious life than non-Brahmins, and any misdeed carries a heavier penalty for them than for lower castes.

In Sanskrit the word for caste is *varna*, which means color. The Brahmins are probably descendants of the light-skinned Aryans who conquered India, and even today the Brahmin's skin is generally several shades lighter than that of other castes.

caste   A doctrine probably devised by the Aryan founders of Hinduism in order to keep the dark-skinned Dravidians they conquered in quiet subjection. It was taught that the four castes—Brahmin, Kshatriya, Vaisya, and Sudra—originally came from four parts of the body of Brahma, the Brahmins from the head and the others from progressively lower parts. The doctrines of karma and reincarnation followed naturally, teaching that those of lower castes by accepting their lot in life uncomplainingly could improve their karma and thus hope for a higher reincarnation the next time around.

The Untouchables were below caste and thus outside the religious system of Hinduism. When the Muslims invaded India, the Untouchables were the easiest to convert, since Islam offered them immediate status. Most of the Christians in India are also descended from Untouchables, many being Christians in name only to raise themselves from Untouchability.

chanan   A soft, aromatic sandalwood paste used to make caste marks and ritualistic marks for religious purposes on both gods and worshipers, generally on the forehead and/or the neck.

Dakshina   One of the many names of Shiva, meaning literally "on the right" and therefore applied to money given to Brahmins as an offering, which must be extended by the right hand.

devatas   The deities or gods.

deya   A small clay cup with a flared lip usually containing ghee or some other oil and a wick, to be lit during religious ceremonies and special celebrations.

dharma   The right way of living for a Hindu. Not an absolute, it varies not only for each caste but also for each person and must be discovered by each individual for himself. Not a moral principle, it involves certain disciplines which supposedly lead the person to a mystical union with Brahman, but which do not necessarily relate consistently to the moral recognition of right and wrong inherent in the human conscience. One's dharma, in fact, could be above right and wrong.

dhoti A long length of cloth which a man wraps around himself like a skirt. Ordinarily it hangs nearly to the ground, but in hot weather or while performing rigorous tasks he may tuck the hem into the waist, cutting the length in half. Some pull the last few feet of the cloth up between their legs, turning the skirt into baggy pants.

Although in the cities many Indians now wear Western clothes, the dhoti is still common in the villages. Even in the cities, holy men and priests generally wear a dhoti, often topped off with a suit jacket.

ghat A special area designated for ceremonial cremation of human bodies. There are many such places throughout India, but the most popular and sacred are near certain "holy" cities, such as Benares, along the banks of the Ganges, making it more convenient to sprinkle the ashes in the sacred river.

ghee Oil made from butter fat, used for ceremonial purposes and considered to be very holy because it comes from the cow, holiest of all creatures.

guru Literally a teacher, but in the sense of being a manifestation of Brahman. Technically the Hindu scriptures cannot be learned just by reading them but must be taught by a guru who himself has learned at the feet of a guru. Every Hindu must follow a guru in order to reach Self-realization. It is through the gurus that the ancient wisdom of the sages passes down to succeeding generations. (Many students of the Bible find a striking connection between this concept of spiritual enlightenment through knowledge and the Tree of Knowledge that brought about the fall of man in the Garden of Eden.)

The guru is worshiped even after his death and is thought by many Hindus to communicate with them more strongly than ever when he has passed from this life to supposedly higher planes of existence. The burial place of a guru is therefore thought by many to be an ideal place for meditation.

higher consciousness There are various "levels" of consciousness opened up in Yoga and meditation, called "higher" states because they differ from one's normal consciousness and are supposedly experienced on the road to nirvana. Different schools of Eastern mysticism define them in different ways. Typical states would be "unity-consciousness," where one experiences a mystical union with the universe, and "God-consciousness," where one experiences that he himself is actually God.

Similar "states of consciousness" are experienced through hypnosis, mediumistic trance, certain drugs, witchcraft ceremonies, voodoo, etc., and all seem to be slight variations of the same occult phenomenon.

Hinduism   The major religion of India, which encompasses so many diverse and contradictory beliefs that it is impossible to define. One could be a pantheist, polytheist, monotheist, agnostic, or even an atheist; a moralist or amoral; a dualist, pluralist, or monist; regular in attendance at temples and in devotion to various gods, or not attend to religious duties at all—and still be called a Hindu.

Hinduism claims to embrace and accept all religious beliefs, but any religion so included becomes part of Hinduism. The syncretist attempts to place Christianity in this "embrace that smothers," but it is clear that the God of the Bible is not Brahman, that heaven is not nirvana, that Jesus Christ is not just another reincarnation of Vishnu, and that salvation through God's grace and faith in Christ's death for our sins and resurrection contradicts the whole teaching of Hinduism.

janma   One name given to a prior life by those who believe in reincarnation. It is used in the sense of a stepping-stone along the path of existence that has prepared one to take the next step. One janma determines what the next janma will be.

jivan-mukti   Highly praised in the *Bhagavad-Gita* as the highest ideal of man, it is the attainment, through Yoga, while still in the body, of mystical union with Brahman.

karma   For the Hindu, the Ultimate Law of destiny or fate. The doctrine teaches that for every moral or spiritual thought, word, or deed, karma produces an inevitable effect. Presumably this could not be carried out in one life; thus karma necessitates reincarnation. The circumstances and conditions of each successive birth and the events of each successive life are supposedly determined absolutely by one's conduct at the same age in past lives. There is no forgiveness in karma. Each must suffer for his own deeds.

Krishna   The most popular and beloved Hindu god and the subject of countless legends, many of them erotic. Krishna is the best-known of the Hindu gods in the West because of the missionary zeal of the singing, dancing, saffron-robed "Hare Krishna" disciples seen in most major cities. They hope to achieve happiness and salvation through chanting over and over the mantra: "Hare Krishna, Hare Krishna, Hare Rama, Hare Rama, Hare Hare Hare." Like Rama, Krishna is presumed to be one of the reincarnations of Vishnu.

kundalini   Literally "coiled," the name of a goddess symbolized by a serpent with three and one half coils, sleeping with its tail in its mouth. This goddess, or "serpent of life, fire, and wisdom," supposedly resides in the body of man near the base of the spine. When aroused without proper control, it rages like a vicious serpent inside of man with a force that is impossible to resist.

It is said that without proper control, the *kundalini* will produce supernatural psychic powers having their source in demonic beings and will lead ultimately to moral, spiritual, and physical destruction. Nevertheless, it is this *kundalini* power that meditation and Yoga are designed to arouse and control. Advanced students of TM and other forms of meditation now practiced in the West have had *kundalini* experiences.

lingam   A term used for the phallic emblem of the god Shiva. There is evidence of lingam worship in the Indus valley predating the Aryan invasion. At first ridiculed by the Aryan conquerors, the worship of this erotic symbol was later adopted by them. Although it is associated with fertility cults, Tantrism, and religious rituals involving sexual perversions, the Shiva lingam is a prominent object of worship in almost every Hindu temple, not only those devoted specifically to Shiva.

lota   A small, brass cup from which "holy" water is poured or sprinkled or drunk in various religious ceremonies.

Mahabharata   One of the two great epic poems of Hindu scriptures, the other one being the *Ramayana*. Consisting of 110 thousand couplets, it is three times as long as the Christian Bible and thus the longest poem in the world. It was the work of numerous poets and editors, who constantly made additions, deletions, and adjustments to suit themselves. Its doctrines are incoherent and often flagrantly contradictory; nevertheless, it is still revered as scripture by Hindus.

mandir   Another word for a Hindu temple.

mantra   A sound symbol of one or more syllables often used to induce a mystical state. It must be passed on by the living voice of a guru and cannot be learned in another way. One need not understand the meaning of the mantra; the virtue is in repetition of the sound. It is said to embody a spirit or deity, and the repetition of the mantra calls this being to the one repeating it. Thus the mantra both invites a particular being to enter the one using it and also creates the passive state in the meditator to facilitate this fusion of beings.

maya   The Hindu explanation for the apparent existence of the entire universe of both mind and body as man experiences it. Since Brahman is the only Reality, all else is illusion, proceeding from Brahma the Creator as heat from a fire. Man's ignorance fails to see the One Reality and thus accepts the illusion or unreal universe of forms and pain and sorrow. Salvation comes through enlightenment dispelling this illusion.

Since the universe appears the same to all observers and follows definite laws, some Hindu sects teach that maya is really a dream of the gods and that men only add their personal sense of suffering.

meditation   To the Westerner this signifies rational contemplation, but to the Eastern mystic it is just the opposite, causing considerable confusion on this subject in the West.

Eastern meditation (being taught as TM, Zen, etc.) is a technique for detaching oneself from the world of things and ideas (from maya) through freeing one's mind from all voluntary or rational thought, which projects one into "higher" states of consciousness.

Though popularized in the West under many names, the aim of all Eastern meditation is to "realize" one's essential union with the Universe. It is the doorway to the "nothingness" called nirvana. Generally sold as a "relaxation" technique, meditation really aims at and ultimately leads to the surrender of oneself to mystical cosmic forces.

moksha Liberation from the cycle of reincarnation through entrance into the ultimate state of being achieved by those who have escaped the universe of maya to arrive at union with Brahman. Hindus look forward to moksha as the end of the pain and suffering reincarnation has imposed upon them through life after life. However, according to orthodox Hinduism, there is no ultimate escape, and one must eventually return to the cycle of deaths and rebirths again. Since at one time there was only Brahman, according to the Hindu scriptures, it will do no good to return to it; moksha is merely a temporary rest, another stage on the "wheel" of existence that goes round and round endlessly, repeating itself every 4.32 billion years.

namahste A common Hindu greeting that to some means simply "hello," it accompanies clasped hands and a polite bow in recognition of the Universal Self within all men.

nirvana Literally a "blowing-out," as to extinguish a candle. Nirvana is "heaven" to both Hindu and Buddhist, although the many sects have different ideas of what it is and how to reach it. Supposedly it is neither a place nor a state and is within us all, waiting to be "realized." It is nothingness, the bliss that comes from no longer being able to feel either pain or pleasure, through the extinction of personal existence by absorption into pure Being.

nyasa The ceremonial act of calling a deity into the worshiper's body by placing one's hands upon forehead, arms, and chest, etc., while repeating a mantra. The repetition of the mantra is itself designed to transform the worshiper into the likeness of the deity embodied in the vibration or sound of the mantra. Nyasa is intended to strengthen this process.

obeah man The Hindu equivalent of a witch doctor, generally understood to have at his command the powers of demons and other lower entities, which he uses, for a fee, to accomplish the wishes of those coming to him for help.

puja Literally "adoration." Both the word and the form of worship it is applied to are of Dravidian origin. It was adopted as the term for all ritualistic and ceremonial worship as the Aryan custom of animal sacrifice, including smearing the altar with blood, gradually gave way in later years under the Buddhist challenge of nonviolence to the Dravidian practice of offering flowers and marking the worshipers with sandal-wood paste.

Along with flowers, modern forms of the Hindu *puja*, performed both in temples and in private homes, generally include offerings of fruit, cloth, water, and money.

pundit   A Brahmin who is especially learned in Hinduism and who is able to apply this knowledge for the benefit of others, such as through advice about the future or intercession with the gods. Not all Brahmins are priests or pundits. Although every Brahmin is automatically qualified by birth, not all devote themselves enough to their religion to become pundits, and most Brahmins in India today follow other professions.

Rama   The reincarnation of Vishnu, whose life is the subject of the epic *Ramayana*. To the Hindu, Rama always acts with the utmost nobility and is the ideal man; his wife, Sita, the ideal woman. Each Hindu sect highly reveres Rama, and his name is the one most commonly given to Indian children. All Hindus would like to die with Rama's name on their lips. When he fell, mortally wounded by his Hindu assassin, Mahatma Gandhi murmured, "O Rama! O Rama!"

Ramayana   Literally "the goings of Rama," one of the two great Hindu epic poems, consisting of seven books relating the human life of the god Rama, a reincarnation of Vishnu. Probably strongly influenced by Buddhist editors, it was originally in several versions; today, three official versions, each varying from the others in some details, are popularly recognized in India.

Rigveda   The most important and revered of the four Vedas (but not the oldest), a collection of miscellaneous old legends, chants (mantras), and hymns, divided into ten books. Its hymns, generally stereotyped and dry, sound the praises of many primitive nature gods. Its priestly prayers are of a selfish and sensual nature, seldom expressing the desire for spiritual wisdom but rather for wine, women, wealth, and power.

sandhya   The god of twilight, a name also given to the morning, noon, and evening prayers of the twice-born Hindu (of castes above Sudra), during which the Gayatri mantra must be repeated as many times as possible, to keep the sun in the sky and to bring salvation to the one chanting it.

sanyasi   A religious Hindu in the fourth stage of life who, having renounced everything, is now above all rules and ritual and holds himself aloof from society and ceremony. If he does not belong to any special order but is independent, he may be called a sadhu—or he could be called a Yogi if he is a master of Yoga.

Self-realization   The ultimate goal of Eastern meditation and Yoga by whatever name it is called: deliverance from the "illusion" that the individual self is different from the Universal Self, or Brahman. Through ignorance man has supposedly forgotten who he really is and thus thinks of himself as distinct from his neighbor and Brahman. Through Self-realization he is liberated from this ignorance of individual existence and returns to Union with Brahman again.

Shakti pat   A term used for the touch of a guru, usually of his hand to the worshiper's forehead, that produces supernatural effects. Shakti literally means power; and in administering the Shakti pat the guru becomes a channel of primal power, the cosmic power underlying the universe, embodied in the goddess Shakti, the consort of Shiva. The supernatural effect of Shakti through the guru's touch may knock the worshiper to the floor, or he may see a bright light and receive an experience of enlightenment or inner illumination, or have some other mystical or psychic experience.

swami   A sanyasi or yogi who belongs to a particular religious order. In practice the term is often applied as a title to the guru or head of the order.

tassas   Large ceremonial drums.

Upanishads   Literally "near-sitting," the name given to a part of the Hindu scriptures that embodies certain mystical teachings that were supposedly originally delivered by ancient gurus to chosen pupils allowed to sit near them for instruction. Dating from about 400 B.C. and originally not considered to be a part of the Vedic canon, the Upanishads have been accepted as such in more recent times.

The Upanishadic philosophy is esoteric and understood by

few. Covering a variety of knotty subjects from the nature of God and man to the purpose of existence and ultimate salvation, the Upanishads try to solve everything with one thesis which runs pretty much through them all: the identity of the individual soul (atman) with the Universal Soul (Brahman), and the essential oneness of everything. One of the most famous expressions of this doctrine is found in the teaching of Uddalaka to his son Svetaketu in the Chandogya Upanishad: "the subtle essence is universally diffused in all things wherever found. It is the true Self; and, Svetaketu, that thou art!"

Vedanta Literally "the ultimate or last or best of the Vedas." In its broadest sense it applies to the Upanishads; in a narrower meaning it refers to one of six orthodox systems of Hindu philosophy based upon the Upanishads and first formulated by the philosopher Bodarayana, who lived about 2,000 years ago. Vedanta is uncompromising in its monistic and pantheistic views; Brahman is All and the only Reality, all else is illusion.

The Vedanta Society, founded by Vivekananda, the successor of Ramakrishna, with centers around the world, professes to teach tolerance for all religions. However, the "unity of all religions" it espouses is really not liberal or broadminded but based upon this uncompromising monism which says everything is One.

Vedas The primary scriptures of Hinduism, said to be greater than the gods because they will endure even when the gods perish. It is believed that they are a revelation from Brahman itself, the Absolute, and existed in their eternal and perfect form from the beginning. The Vedas are Rigveda, Yajurveda, Samaveda, and Atharvaveda. As a whole they have been divided into four classifications: the Mantras (metrical psalms of praise); the Brahmanas (manuals of ritual and prayer for priestly guidance); the Aranyakas (special treatises for hermits and saints); and the Upanishads (philosophical treatises).

Vedic The language in which the Vedas were originally composed, an archaic form of Sanskrit also called Old Indo-Aryan. As an adjective it means "as taught or exemplified in the Vedas."

Yoga Literally, "yoking" and refers to union with Brahman.

There are several kinds and schools of Yoga, and various techniques, but all have this same ultimate goal of union with the Absolute.

The positions and breath control are intended as aids to Eastern meditation, and a means of controlling the body in disciplining oneself to renounce all desires which the body might otherwise impose upon the mind.

Yoga is designed specifically to induce a state of trance which supposedly allows the mind to be drawn upward into a yoking with Brahman. It is a means of withdrawal from the world of illusion to seek the only true Reality. If one desires to achieve physical fitness only, exercises designed for that specific purpose ought rather to be chosen. No part of Yoga can be separated from the philosophy behind it.

Yogi In the loose sense, anyone who has attained some proficiency in the practice of Yoga, but in the true sense, one who is a master of Yoga; that is, one who has attained, through the practice of Yoga, the union with Brahman which is its aim.

The true meditating Yogi has cut himself off from all sense perceptions, including family and friends and all human relationships. He is supposed to be beyond space and time, caste, country, and religion, and even beyond good and evil.

As Krishna said in the *Bhagavad-Gita*, nothing matters anymore to the Yogi except Yoga itself.